THE JOY OF GIVING MASSAGE

HOW TO GIVE A MASSAGE SO GOOD YOU'LL WANT TO DO IT ALL THE TIME

SHAI PLONSKI

Copyright © 2018 by Shai Plonski.

All Rights Reserved.

No part of this book may be reproduced, stored in retrieval systems, or transmitted by any means, electronic, mechanical, photocopying, recorded or otherwise without written permission from the author.

ISBN: 978-1-63161-065-3

Published by TCK Publishing
www.TCKpublishing.com

Get discounts and special deals on our best-selling books at
www.TCKpublishing.com/bookdeals

To sign up for Shai's newsletter or to find out more information about current courses and products offered visit **www.stillightcentre.com**

DISCLAIMER

Read Before Beginning

The information contained in this book is for informational and recreational purposes only and should not be used to replace professional medical advice. People who purchase this book or any related materials are solely responsible for how they choose to utilize this content.

This book and any related materials contained here should not be relied on in diagnosing or treating a medical condition. It is best to seek advice and attention from your physician or qualified healthcare professional. Always consult your physician before beginning a new treatment or fitness program. But with all that in mind, if used for the purposes of promoting and sharing relaxation, kindness, and compassion that respects and honors the abilities and limitations of both you and the person you give to, then get ready for some outstanding results.

CONTENTS

Introduction		ix
Part 1:	Compassionate Touch for a Richer Life	1
	Chapter 1: The Power of Touch	3
	Chapter 2: Planting Seeds	7
	Chapter 3: What Does It Mean to Be on a Spiritual Path?	11
	Chapter 4: Down the Rabbit Hole	19
	Chapter 5: My Shame & Vulnerability	27
	Chapter 6: The Science of Touch	33
	Chapter 7: Shifting from the Head to the Heart	39
Part 2:	Learning Compassionate Touch	47
	Chapter 8: Learning at Home	49
	Chapter 9: The Tools of the Trade	55
	Chapter 10: The First Pillar: Meditation and Metta	61
	Chapter 11: The Second Pillar: Stances	67
	Chapter 12: The Third Pillar: Rocking	75
	Chapter 13: The Fourth Pillar: Touch & the Secrets to Giving an Outstanding Massage	83
	Chapter 14: Communicating Safety & Comfort for an Optimal Massage	105
	Chapter 15: Massage Facing Up	115
	Chapter 16: Massaging Facing Down	125
Part 3:	Love: the Source of Compassionate Touch	139
	Chapter 17: There Are Elephants in the Room	141
	Chapter 18: A Different Kind of Love Letter	145
Part 4:	Student's Stories	149
	Chapter 19: Meet Mary Beth	151
	Chapter 20: Meet Pamyla	155
	Chapter 21: Meet Jeff	159
	Chapter 22: My Voice Is Touch	163
Resources		165
Acknowledgements		167
About the Author		171

For Sophie, my daughter, my teacher, and the coolest person I know

Thank you to my students who have inspired this book and taught me again and again that we are all each other's teachers

"The internal equivalent to oxygen, what we need in order to survive is love… Laws of the universe such as gravity describe the way things are. Faith in them merely shows that we understand what they are… The highest internal law is that we love one another… Human relationships exist to produce love. As surely as a lack of oxygen will kill us, so will a lack of love."

~Marianne Williamson,
Return to Love: Reflections on the Principles of A Course in Miracles

Massage as compassionate touch is a vehicle for sharing the best of our human spirit—both inside and out.

INTRODUCTION

Raise your hand if you've enjoyed receiving a massage at some point in your life. Raise your hand if you'd like to have someone in your life who could give it to you all the time, no strings—or money—attached! Now, raise your hand if the last thing you want to do is actually give massage as a way to get it.

Why do you suppose that is? If I were to take a guess, I'd say that giving massage up till this point in your life has felt like hard and unrewarding work. And at the end of a long day where you might have already lived that experience—be it inside or outside the house—that's the last thing you want to sign up for.

But what if it doesn't have to be that way? What if you could quickly learn some essential secrets to giving a massage that makes BOTH giving and receiving it so darned good you'll want to do it all the time?

What if everything you've ever learned about what a massage is and could be, is in fact wrong? And at the top of that list is that massage is mainly for the person on the receiving end.

I know that's how most of us typically view massage, but that doesn't have to be the case. In fact, you will be learning how to flip that right around.

I didn't write this book primarily so you could make your partner really happy, although you will! I wrote it so you could fall in love with giving it specifically because of what it can do for you.

Joy is in the title because living a joyful life is a pretty good goal to have on the road to living a quality and fulfilling life. The more joy the better! Joy can be a feeling of great pleasure and happiness, but not all feelings of joy are made the same way. You have the kind that comes from eating a delicious piece of chocolate cake or having a nice glass of wine or any number of external pleasures, which are both fun and temporary. As such, they live on the surface of our life.

What's more, you have advertisers, marketers, business people, and the like who know all about that kind of joy and continually find ways to exploit that so we get attached to seeking and spending more money on joyful pleasures.

But there's another kind of joy that I would like you to consider here. The joy that is connected to a well of vital energy that lives inside you. The kind that every time you experience it, you are freeing yourself, because it is timeless, boundless, and does a world of good. When you experience that kind of joy, you feel connected, supported, and the happiness that it brings fills you with gratitude and excitement for simply being alive.

In my opinion, we are each capable of determining which kind of joy we are experiencing at any given moment. The first kind is a quick fix, and the second is long lasting. Experiencing the first kind can inspire you to seek out the second. Filling our lives with more opportunities of that second kind puts us well on the road to living in a way that is happier and more fulfilling.

With all that being said, wouldn't it be amazing if you could experience that long-lasting joy through the simple act of giving a massage? If you could give a massage that could help you feel like that (while also helping someone you care about), wouldn't you want to give it all day long?

I know I would. I feel blessed everyday to have discovered simple and easily accessible methods that are always at my fingertips. And that's what makes me so excited to share the essence of this book. Because you can do it too, and all it takes is one afternoon to get started and feel the benefits.

This Book Is for You

If you're looking for ways to improve your health and well-being as you bring Spirit or God or Love inward, this book is for you. It's also for you if you're looking for an incredible way to strengthen relationships and share all the benefits of your practice with your loved ones, friends, family, and world.

Compassionate touch as a massage form is a missing link that connects you and your deeper truth with your community and environment. It is a way to help you move from your head to your heart. It is one of the pieces of the puzzle toward wholeness and holiness, yet it is often overlooked.

There are millions upon millions of people who are committed toward healthier living who do not know how beneficial giving (and receiving) massage among loved ones can be. Many of you probably already practice some form of yoga, meditation, martial arts, dance, healthy eating, getting into nature, prayer, and/or religion. Your reasons to engage in these practices are as varied as there are people, but at the same time there is a lot of overlap. Reasons include, but are not limited to: being healthy, happy, having outstanding relationships, being connected to a greater purpose, and living a long and high-quality life.

Yet in my experience, even among the most experienced yogis, and long-time meditators, only a small sliver truly understand and are connected to the power of giving massage. The secret I want to share is that compassionate touch is a way to enhance and share the benefits of your personal development. It can radically transform your life—and the lives of those around you—for the better. Whatever your dreams are for a better and healthier life, massage can play a huge part in making them come true.

At the same time, I believe that most of us would agree that our salvation, our way through hard times, and our way to embrace the fun times is in the love, the connections, and the union we establish with one another.

Humans by design are social beings; we need each other in order to evolve and find Love. There are so many great modern spiritual teachers, including Wayne Dyer, Marianne Williamson, Eckhart Tolle, Jon Kabat-Zinn, Pema Chodron, Thich Nhat Hanh, the Dalai Lama, to name just a few. The undercurrent of their message is that the way toward a love-enriched life is to move away from the ego. Our ability to do that and overcome our pain, our suffering, and our roadblocks, is a miracle. And it takes people connecting and joining together to live a miracle. As such, to see love and God in your brother's and sister's eyes—and by extension in your own—is the road to peace. Of course, this is a thought that is often easier said than done. It is one thing to have the concept and quite another to live it and breathe it and manifest it.

That may be especially true these days, in a world that is arguably starved for human contact and for meaningful connections. Bob Dylan sang about this back in 1963 in "Talkin' World War III Blues" where he sings about isolation and loneliness. Back then, computers, smartphones, and the like were still a fantasy. Now? People of all stripes and ages spend so much more of our time engaged in activities that isolate us physically even when they bring us together in cyberspace.

Compassionate touch is the antidote to this way of living and is a powerful tool that helps break down the habits and walls which keep us separate. It is a kind of massage that taps into the energy of the present moment. It is all about abundance, fullness, and joyfulness. Giving this kind of massage helps you to access the love within every cell of your body and gives you a way to share it. This massage has the power to lift the veil of separation, to sense the beauty in your partner, to look beyond their pain and your own. To create a miracle.

It is not performed as a goal or an expectation; it simply happens because that is the power of loving touch. When you connect with another person in this way, stress melts, health returns, and bonds are deepened for you and for them.

This book is meant to inspire, to teach you how to give massage, and to explain the benefits you'll receive from it. Ideally, you'll find at least one person to learn these skills with so that you both get to experience giving and receiving regularly.

Engaging in this kind of massage exchange regularly is like putting money in the bank. During the exchange, you get to experience all the benefits of a great massage—both giving and receiving. Over time, there is also a cumulative effect to your overall health from removing stress, detoxing your body, and connecting with people close to you.

It is not a given that as we age our body has to break down. Chronic pain and stiffness and many of the characteristics often associated with old age can be affected and drastically reduced by the choices we make. One shining example of this is my yoga teacher, Dr. Madan Bali. I met him when he was seventy-six, and he's still going strong at ninety-four, teaching yoga six days a week and sharing his passion. His eyesight and hearing might not be what they once were, but his vitality is as strong as ever.

If you have someone in your life that you can massage with every week for the next year—or ten—how would that change you? How would it change them? If you have a skill that can touch someone on a deeper level, what does that do for your self-confidence, your self-esteem, your energy, and your desire to help others?

If you can receive someone else's compassionate touch on a regular basis, what will that do for your outlook, your stress levels, and your body?

Compassionate touch draws from and feeds the fountain of youth within you; a knowingness that you are connected to something bigger than yourself, a universal and abundant source of energy that you're able to tap into whenever you need it.

Giving massage as compassionate touch teaches you how to access this loving place for yourself and then share it with others. The benefits can be limitless and include your personal health and well-being, both physically and emotionally. It helps in relationships with your friends, families, and romantic partners. It is folk medicine that brings you into contact with Spirit in the most beautiful of ways.

Most of the people I meet in my everyday life love to receive massage. It's the giving they don't like. That is often because they do not understand how much fun it can be when you learn how to do it in such a way that takes care of yourself at the same time as you're helping others. Then it's not tedious work or painful on the hands—it is total play.

I encourage you to make room for compassionate touch in your life. In order to do that, we must find a willingness to let go of something else that is already taking up space in our jam-packed schedules.

That's a big ask, so I'll share why I think that's important and share some of how massage has helped me in my life. In Part One, I peel back some of my layers and background in Thai Massage, to try to bring into words that which often leaves me speechless. The revelation of massage helps you know and heal yourself while helping others and opens up a direct relationship with Spirit.

In Part Two, I will teach you some skills, including the secrets to giving an incredible massage that is at least as good to give as it is to receive. It is something you can learn at home in an afternoon. It is a high-quality, 30-minute massage that you can give to your loved ones right away. It will help both of you feel so good that you'll want to do it all the time.

I walk you through all the steps as if I were personally training you to teach the massage. No stone is left unturned, and all the tools needed to give the massage are readily available and probably in your living room or bedroom as you read.

In Part Three, I share some of my poetry, part of the heart of my practice, and what has inspired me to keep teaching for the past fifteen years.

Part Four shares student stories of how they are using this massage every day, with the aim that you can find a kernel or two of inspiration and identification with other people on this amazing path.

I write this book as a person who has struggled with faith, pain, frustration, and depression. I've asked these larger-life questions for a long time and have been looking for ways forward in my life again and again.

It also happens that I have a young daughter—the coolest person I know—and in many ways, I am writing this book for her. I believe compassionate touch has the power to change her life as much, if not more, than it did mine. My goal for her as she grows older is to know the limitless potential she already has within her. That which she already embodies as a six-year-old should remain with her for her whole life.

I believe that peace, and a track to a better world, is a personal endeavor. It starts within and is shared with those closest to us and then extends outwards. It is built on a bedrock of love, internal forgiveness, and then by extending this energy to those we care about. I would love for my daughter to grow up in a time and place where the norm is people on such a path. Hopefully, these tools will help make that a reality.

This is a deeply personal book, unlike any other I've ever written. I want us to have fun and share from the heart as best we can.

So, without further ado, let's jump in!

PART I

COMPASSIONATE TOUCH FOR A RICHER LIFE

⌘

"For one human being to love another; that is perhaps the most difficult of all our tasks, the ultimate, the last test and proof, the work for which all other work is but preparation."

~RAINER MARIA RILKE

CHAPTER 1

THE POWER OF TOUCH

"Happiness is the daily experience of a meaningful life."

~MAX STROM

Massage between loved ones, friends, and for people in need is the key toward experiencing a full spiritual life. It has the capacity to open us to Love in all its abundance and then becomes a vehicle for sharing that immaculate gift. I am on a mission to share this wisdom and move the needle in that direction.

I have been practicing and teaching Thai Massage since 2002. By now, I have completed thousands of hours of training and teaching this art. But at one point, I was a total newbie. I did not have any prior experience massaging or with the theories behind it. When I first learned to give massage, I learned primarily by hands-on experience, by practicing on friends and loved ones and relying on their feedback to teach me what to do.

It was from that place that I gave and fell in love hard! One of my earliest massages was with a friend of a friend that I had never met. I went to her house, we had a short greeting, and then I set to work. In those last fifteen minutes of the session, I felt so connected to this person, who was essentially a stranger. Time felt like it had stopped as we got a taste of how connected we were. What's more, as we shared a tea afterwards, she expressed the exact same experience. A bond had been made with someone I never knew previously and have never seen again.

Since then I have taught more than 3,300 people the art of Thai Massage. Some of my students are already massage professionals or yoga teachers when they come into my classes. They want to learn in order to add another skill to their tool belt, but plenty are not. They are couples, they are mother and daughter, father and son. They have elderly friends, children, and extended families they want to share with. They know someone dying of cancer, someone suffering in some way. They are frustrated and want to help. I have taught people as young as twelve and as old as eight-five. I have massaged people as young as a few weeks and as old as ninety-three.

They come to learn a technique and they are all—every single one of them—amazed by how much more they get from the class than that.

> **Bonds are formed, tears are shed, lives are transformed by what it means to connect through touch.**

I feel guided and compelled to share the message of this book because of my first-hand knowledge and that of my students of the incredible ways giving massage as compassionate touch helps. It helps you and those you touch in ways beyond words.

One of the essential things I have learned is that the word *massage* is a term of convenience. It is an umbrella term, and it means many things to many people.

In a Thai Massage people keep their clothes on, and it is performed on a mat on the ground just as often as it's done on a table. Really though, it can be done anywhere, including on a bed, sitting in a chair, even standing in line waiting for a table at your favorite restaurant.

Thai Massage emanates from the heart outward. It is all about giving from and with the best of the human spirit. You make a conscious effort in Thai Massage toward mindfulness, toward paying attention to yourself, to your partners, and to what it means to be present. You are not always successful, and that is less important. You try to forgive yourself when you find you are lost in thoughts of the past and future, and then you come back to your breath and begin again.

At its core, the way I practice and teach, a Thai Massage is as good to give as it is to receive. If you've ever received a really good Thai Massage, then you may already know what many have told me after I've finished working with them.

Comments like, "I feel two inches taller" or "ten years younger." Like, "You got rid of stress and tension that I didn't even know I was carrying" and "I have been to see a physiotherapist, chiropractor, other massage therapists, you name it, but this was totally different. You released what none of the others could." These comments are part of the norm.

Giving a massage needs to feel at least as good as that. At least equal amounts of time are spent on how you feel giving the massage, which helps your partner to enjoy it and release her tensions that much more. If it doesn't, then what's the point? Why would you want to give it? Why would you want to make some important changes in your life to allow room for regular exchanges if it wasn't that good? How could it be part of your spiritual life and practice?

You'll notice I've used the term Thai Massage. That's because the roots of this form are in Thai Massage as it was taught to me. But it is a term of convenience, and if you've been to Thailand, and had a session with someone in your Western neighborhood, the experiences would likely be different from one another. There are as many kinds of Thai Massage as there are people who give them. What's more, not every Thai Massage is going to feel good, because not everyone gives with the heart and pays attention with that loving intention.

Furthermore, there are many kinds of massage and many different kinds of massage therapists who massage from their heart center. Breema and Tao Shiatsu are just two modalities that operate from similar meditative principles. You can also find people giving Swedish, deep-tissue, or any modality who give from a heart-centered approach.

What this book is about—and what I'm really trying to introduce you to—is the skill and the idea of giving compassionate touch. It could involve some kind of squeezing, searching for, and releasing knots of tension. It may mean getting energy moving in the body and helping to put someone in guided stretches or some combination of all of the above. Alternatively, it doesn't have to include any of those aspects, except the part that your heart guides you, and you are making a conscious choice to connect with another person through loving touch. While you massage, you should always return to the principle that it should feel as good to give as it does to receive.

Whether you call it Thai Massage, Thai Yoga Massage, Thai Yoga Therapy, compassionate touch, or simply massage, I am asking you to learn a heart-centered massage. It is intuitive, fun, and should feel great to give and receive. At the core though, this massage is about sharing loving kindness and compassion as a form of bodywork.

Giving massage is about all the benefits experienced between two people in the moment, but it can be so much more than that. And when you're giving massage, your ability to help and provide support to your partner is a bonus. But first and foremost is how much you are helping yourself.

CHAPTER 2

PLANTING SEEDS

"If you are distressed by anything external, the pain is not due to the thing itself, but your estimate of it. This you have the power to remove at any time."

~MARCUS AURELIUS

Thai Massage has been practiced in Thailand for 2,000 years, and its origins can be traced back to India 2,500 years ago during the time of the Buddha.

The founder of Thai Massage was an Indian (ayurvedic) doctor by the name of Dr. Jivaka Kumar Bhaccha. He was a revered, well-known healer, and I heard of him long before I ever heard about Thai Massage.

That's because I read the book *Old Path White Clouds* by Thich Nhat Hanh, which is a retelling of the Buddha's life through the eyes of a boy who tended buffaloes. It is built from ancient texts that captured some of the Buddha's life. That story includes Jivaka, who was the Buddha's physician, and he also donated part of his property to the Buddha and his community (the sangha) for retreats whenever the Buddha toured through that part of India.

For the most part, Buddhism was lost to India for thousands of years, and only returned en masse when Tibetan exiles made India their home in the twentieth century. Buddhism flourished when it left India 2,000 years ago and went east to places like China, Japan, and Thailand. And to this day, 95% of the Thai population identifies as Buddhist.

Thai Massage went along for the ride and, in many ways, the Thai people were simply way ahead of the West regarding the value and role that massage can play in one's overall healthcare.

In Thailand, Thai Massage (Nuad Boran or ancient massage) is a folk art. That means that someone in the family learned how to give the massage and would massage all their family members, and then pass it on to the next generation.

What the Thai people learned long ago is that massage is best practiced in the home, and that it is one way to cultivate one's spiritual practice and to help take care of loved ones. In fact, these two things are considered one and the same.

Massage as it is practiced in Thailand is preventative medicine. You don't wait until you get sick or feel pain to give or receive a massage. You give it and you get it because you are feeling good and you want to keep feeling good.

What a radical notion! It is an idea whose time has come. Imagine how your life would change if these were part of the choices you got to make with your intimate partner, friends, and family? How much better would you and your partner(s) feel on a daily basis? How much less would you have to visit a doctor? How would that impact your relationships, your ability to communicate, your ability to sense the other person? How much of an effect could that have on the rest of your life and with the people you meet beyond the exchange of compassionate touch?

Every so often I have students in my classes who are raised in these kinds of households in the West, and it always warms my heart. They tell the story of how giving massage was a daily family activity, and how it was simply a part of growing up. It was only once they got to high school and beyond that they realized that not every family operated that way. What's more, their house was a place where friends wanted to be, so that they, too, could be part of this exchange because of the closeness and the relationships this fostered among loved ones.

It's all pretty sweet and attainable if you want to bring this into your life and community. At the very least, having the willingness and excitement to learn is the starting point. At the same time, it's not that simple for most of us, as there are constant starts and stops to bringing healthy activity into our lives. We may have the best of intentions to make healthy changes, but it doesn't always work.

So how do you make it work? How do you learn the skills of compassionate touch and then make room for it in your life?

When it comes to most of what I teach, you will discover that you already know what to do.

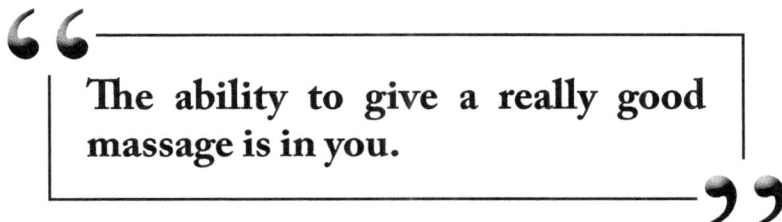

> **The ability to give a really good massage is in you.**

As for the rest, we take one step at a time to practice at a high level in little time. The first step is learning the skills, but beyond that, it is at least as important to make space for a regular massage exchange in your life.

The best advice I ever got about change is that you have to commit to one month of dedicated change. It's all about getting something off the ground, and once this takes root you'll have it. It's yours. For example, if your goal is to exchange compassionate touch two times a week—once to give and once to receive—then that's what you need to do for a month.

The good news about Thai Massage—or compassionate touch—is that it can be shared in so many different contexts with just about anyone. It also counts if you don't have anyone to practice on, but simply wish to engage in it in some way. That could involve reading through the techniques shared here or visualizing yourself giving the massage or even imagining that person in front of you and going through the steps of giving that massage.

We'll explore all of this and more in the coming chapters to develop and cultivate the habits of change.

CHAPTER 3

WHAT DOES IT MEAN TO BE ON A SPIRITUAL PATH?

"Letting there be room for not knowing is the most important thing of all. When there's a big disappointment, we don't know if that's the end of the story. It may just be the beginning of a great adventure. Life is like that. We don't know anything. We call something bad; we call it good. But really we just don't know."

~PEMA CHODRON,
WHEN THINGS FALL APART:
HEART ADVICE FOR DIFFICULT TIMES

This chapter is a collaborative effort. I cannot pretend to know what it means for you to be on a spiritual path. I would love to hear from you so we can expand on these words and share our collective story and speak it to more and more people.

I don't recall ever making a conscious decision to start on a more spiritual path. I grew up in a Jewish household, and I remember having the politics and the meaning of religion forced onto me. As such, God and religion were always things to question. I celebrated the Sabbath most weeks and went to synagogue on the most religious holidays until I was about eight. I attended Jewish school until I was twelve and had a bar mitzvah when I was thirteen.

As an adult, I still celebrate the holidays every year, including a fast on the Day of Atonement (Yom Kippur), honoring the New Year, and keeping Passover (refraining from eating leavened foods for eight days). I do it to remember where I come from, and because family remains important to me. These connections keep me in touch with my loved ones and those roots. Judaism remains a part of me, but it only goes so deep. The religion itself—along with organized religion in general—is something that I do not relate to at my core.

In needing to fill that void, I set out to question just about everything, starting with the meaning of life and my place in it. I was also obsessed with death from age six. For about six years, at some point in any given day, I would have some kind of panic attack where my thoughts would turn to dying and not being in and of this world anymore.

The start of my spiritual journey began there, from a deep need to make sense of my fears of dying and to stop that sense of dread every day. It was this thought that eventually permeated into my consciousness: "It is okay not to know the answer."

As such, it was the start of my journey in getting comfortable with not knowing all of the answers to my questions, and that *unknowingness* being perfectly acceptable. Eventually, I learned that it was more than okay. It was a fruitful and vital way to get comfortable in my own skin. By accepting the space of not knowing, I have learned to empty myself of the expectation that I need to know the answers to my biggest questions, fears, and hopes this very instant. That has helped me to remain open, to receive. These choices were how I first came to have faith. Faith in something bigger than myself and the testing of faith that comes by maintaining a belief in God or Spirit or Love, even when life kept coming at me in hard, frustrating, and confusing ways.

Now I see that one of the laws of the universe is that this space of unknowingness does get filled up. Answers and opportunities in life do come, in many unexpected ways. It took time, but eventually I knew a few things. As long as I don't get too attached to those thoughts, I've found that's a pretty good place from which to live. This balancing act reminds me of a song by Nahko and Medicine for the People called "Black as Night." They sing about the limits of knowing and not knowing.

Pursuing a spiritual path in earnest may have been happening my whole life, but it really became conscious when I was seventeen, out of high school, and onto the next level of education. The testing, the questioning, the desire to expand my mind and expose myself to new ideas and life experiences was central to how I lived my life. A couple of years later, this pursuit took off when my girlfriend at the time presented me with my first journal. There I had an outlet, a way to channel all the confusion in my head onto the page. (Melanie, wherever you may be, thank you!). From nineteen until twenty-five, I filled journal after journal with the testing of faith that was happening on most days. My head was full of questions and often feelings of self-pity whenever it seemed that life repeated itself in patterns that I thought I had already learned the answers to.

I was knocked down so many times I lost count. I was frustrated often, depressed regularly, feeling like I was back to square one. Each time, though, I realized that it felt (and still feels) like a test. The questions "What is there to learn here?" and "Do I still have faith in Spirit and myself?" would ring in my head. If I felt my heart broken for whatever reason, would that be a reason to harden my shell, to increase my cynicism, and to protect myself from future heartbreak? Or to soften and continue?

On a conscious level, I knew the answer was to lean into the latter, to surrender, to make sure that the child-like spirit in me was given room at the table of life. On a subconscious level, I am less certain that has always been the choice I've been making. That shell has continued to harden and grow into a pretty thick wall, and learning how to trust has and will always be part of my life's work. At the same time, at least I knew how important it was not to lose faith.

One of the bigger life changes that opened up the door for me was learning from other people, other teachers. The role they play in my life is dramatically different from what I used to believe. I used to think that any progress on a spiritual path had to be alone and that other people weren't part of that journey. Part of my thinking went like this: "It is great that the Buddha found his way and his enlightenment, but he found what worked for him, just like I need to do for myself."

I spent a lot of time in my late teens and early twenties believing that with all my heart.

That all changed when I went on my first Vipassana meditation retreat in the Goenka style. Vipassana meditation is said to be the technique that the Buddha used to achieve his enlightenment. It uses breath as a method for doing the deep, inner work of getting to know oneself and one's inner universe. When we commit to a ten-day retreat, we're signing up for total silence. We meditate for ten hours a day, and the rest of the time we are not supposed to speak or make eye contact with anyone else, except if we have questions for the facilitator. The purpose is to dedicate our entire time to the technique, to observe oneself, the changes taking place, and to be able to see how it works for ourselves.

I always say those ten days of silence—of looking inward with such precision and purpose—were both the most fulfilling and most difficult days of my life. It changed me forever, especially regarding the solo journey. I already meditated a bit, had been doing yoga for a few years, and had been looking for more meaning in my life for a long time. This course helped take everything I had been pursuing and living and took it to another level. It crystallized things and gave me clarity.

There was pain and suffering and hurt that came up in those ten days that I didn't realize I was still holding onto. Observing those sensations and then doing my best not to react meant that I could let go of some of my suffering and could witness that process in action. Vipassana showed me that whatever hardships, challenges, and growth spurts to come, I would have a technique to fall back on.

Although I do not currently maintain a regular Vipassana practice, it taught me the value and importance of great teachers in my life. Since then, I stop, think, and appreciate how much people have to offer one another, how we are all each other's teachers. Not only is doing it alone lonely, but it is dead-end thinking. And it just isn't true. We are all dialed in to shared energy and a shared life. If an idea or insight comes through me, it is an illusion to think that it is mine or that I owned it and birthed it. It is collective, because we are all connected.

Teachers and well-established practices have tremendous value to help open the doors to life. And we find these teachers everywhere. Yes, there are formal courses we sign up for, but teachers are all around us and certainly in every person we care about deeply.

It is likely no accident that shortly after I completed my Vipassana course I would discover and fall head over heels with Thai Massage. At that time, I was meditating regularly for a couple hours a day, and I was delighted by the results on my psyche and my relationship to the present moment. That taste was getting sweeter every day, but I could also sense the need to share the benefits of this practice.

When I was twenty-six, I went to a retreat center called the Omega Institute in Rhinebeck, New York to volunteer for the summer and meet people who were in a similar place as I was. People who were also actively searching for deeper meaning in their lives and sharing the fruits of their discoveries. One of the first friends I made was a Thai Massage practitioner teaching a short workshop to the staff, Kaline Kelly. I was blown away when she told me that at the root level the massage is about shared Vipassana meditation. That is, it is a way to train the giver in how to come into the present moment and to connect with another person through loving kindness and compassion. The massage therefore needs to feel at least as good to give as it is to receive.

Those words have remained with me until this day. They've been the guiding force for how I have tried to learn, both from my mentors and through my practice. They are at the core of everything I've shared with my students and my way of giving back to this timeless and beautiful healing art.

I also discovered at Omega that one of the original North American Thai Massage teachers lived in Montreal, a Malaysian man named Kam Thye Chow. He had spent six years in Thailand studying with his master, Asokananda, but love and fate had brought him to Canada, of all places. What's more, he lived only two blocks away from me.

I sought him out with very little money, a thirst to learn, and the willingness to contribute to his school however I could. We clicked on many levels and, within a year, I was well on the path to teaching. In short order, I became the manager of the school and helped implement the curriculum and write the books for teacher training and advanced level courses.

It was a relationship that served us both well for many years, and it is where I learned the foundation of this craft. Over the nine years we spent together there were many ups and downs as. Unfortunately, things did not end as I would have wished. Those subconscious walls I spoke of—and which I'll speak of in Chapter Five—definitely played their part in that less-than-ideal ending to our relationship.

The way I see things now…

> **Having meaningful connections and seeing growth in my relationships is usually the best sign that I'm making progress on a spiritual path.**

It is in my relationships that I am freed from much of my suffering. My relationships are often a reflection of either my stubborn desire to be right or of letting go and find something else, which is love. I do that by being vulnerable and sharing what's in my heart, and through a willingness to let go of things that cannot be resolved with someone who thinks they are just as right as I am. Instead, I focus on being authentic. More often than not, it's been my ability (or inability) to do that that becomes a reflection of where I'm at in any given moment.

Mary Oliver, a revered poet, said this when asked about what it means for her to be more spiritual: "I've become kinder, more people-oriented, and willing to grow old. I was always interested in everlasting life and am a little more interested now and a little more content with my answers."

Poet and artist Flavia Weedin, who died in 2015, had this to say: "Some people come into our lives and move our souls to dance. They awaken us to understanding with the passing whisper of their wisdom.…They make our world more beautiful, leave footprints in our hearts, and we are never ever the same."

Her daughter had this to share in Weedin's obituary: "Flavia knew that in small things there existed great virtues. Mama's wealth was her capacity to love. Indeed, she was the richest woman among us.… Her voice reminded us that we are never alone. More than anything Mama believed in love…and it was from her we learned how to find beauty in the ordinary. It was from her we all learned that giving love is life's greatest gift.… In Flavia's own words, 'If I could sit across the porch from God, I'd thank him for lending me you.'"

I am forever grateful to Wayne Dyer and the many words of wisdom and teachings he has shared. In his book *I Can See Clearly Now*, he had this to say about spirituality:

> *"Shift from ego to meaning. The primary inner desire is serving others and creating a world where God realization is a universal reality.... Spirituality isn't about manifesting what you want, it's about manifesting what you are.... All of my wants for things come from a consciousness of lack.... Instead understand that I am already whole and complete and that the process of manifestation is about becoming all that I intended to be—reclaiming my divinity, my connection to source.... Dwelling day by day in thoughts of peace and love toward every creature is the path of awareness that leads to abounding peace."*

I've come to realize that all the trials, tribulations, and celebrations are training in how to love and allow that to be the cornerstone of my life. Those patterns that seem on auto repeat keep coming to me, so I can learn something more about what it means to love with all my heart and every fiber of my being. I am still a beginner at this and will be for the rest of my life.

Here is what it means to me at this particular point in time to be on a spiritual path.

It includes being dedicated to:

- Living a better life
- Surrendering to Spirit or God
- Living a life of service
- Letting go of ego's grip
- Wanting to be happy and feeling happiness in every fiber of my being
- Pursuing my deepest dreams for a fulfilling life
- Doing a regular practice, which these days includes a mix of self-massage, yoga, meditation, hiking, and rollerblading
- Making more meaningful connections with everyone in my life, especially the people I love and care about most
- Exploring and embracing what it means to be empathetic and supportive
- Asking for forgiveness
- Embracing the role of vulnerability and leaning into it as a way to accomplish all of the above

So, I ask you… "What does it mean to you to be on a spiritual path?"

CHAPTER 4

DOWN THE RABBIT HOLE

"Forgiveness is the fragrance that the violet sheds on the heel that crushed it."

~MARK TWAIN

What do you want to be when you grow up? This classic question has been with me for as long as I can remember.

Those words have tortured me a whole lot more than they've ever helped. No matter what I was doing, no matter how much I enjoyed life, the answer had always been "I don't know." Not that I would let that confusion get in the way of a good adventure and its accompanying story. In fact, one of the benefits of not knowing the answer to that question is that when I'm in the right frame of mind, I stop trying to find the answer. I have always gotten a lot farther and have had the best and most memorable experiences from giving in, from forgetting the question and simply living the answer.

There was the time, for example, when I found myself travelling on my own in Tokyo, Japan, lost in the middle of the night. It forced me to give in to moment and trust in the journey.

I had long had a burning desire to visit this part of the world, but the places that really attracted me were China and India. Tai Chi was already a huge passion of mine, and yoga wasn't far behind. When it came to Japan, I knew nothing about it except that my twin sister was there, and as a Canadian I could get a working-holiday visa. It was a nice set-up, so the Land of the Rising Sun would be my springboard into the East.

My first view of the countryside, taking an early January train from Osaka airport to Komatsu City in the Ishikawa region, was gray, rainy, and dreary. The only thought I remember from that first impression is "What am I doing here?"

The answer, after nearly two straight days of travel, was that I would step off that train and go directly with my sister to an extracurricular activity. It was a Wednesday when I arrived, and she was teaching an evening English class in the local community center. The students were mostly housewives looking for a cultural experience, and it was an easy way for her to make a few extra yen.

On this night, me and my long, brown curly hair would serve as the main attraction. And it didn't take long for my exhaustion to lift as I sat in that class and patiently answered their questions.

These women, with their gentle probing and kind laughter, gave me my second impression of Japan. And apparently, it was something I was dying to learn.

Although they could barely speak a full sentence in English, and I still couldn't bring a word of Japanese to the surface, the message was soft and fuzzy. It filtered through my haze, my defenses, my wall, and after enough repetition over those weeks and months, it's fair to say that eventually it came through loud and clear.

That fateful night in Tokyo came about two months after I had first stepped foot in the country. By then I had considered my landlord Shoda-san to be my Japanese mother.

She owned the house that my sister and I called home in the Japanese countryside. It was a simple dwelling that we had managed to turn upside down and inside out, leaving our mark and our clothes everywhere.

Whatever mess we made, she didn't care. She had taken us in and opened my eyes wide. I had already learned so much from her, from her actions, her calm and gentle demeanor, the casual way in which she helped, and what it felt like to be in her company.

What's more, her son lived in Tokyo, which gave me a landing place from which to explore the city.

I arrived in the center of town the night before and met up with our landlord's son, Yoshitada Shoda. We first met in the evening in central Tokyo as I rolled in and he was finishing work. It took three trains and about an hour and a half to get to his matchbox-sized apartment with its kitchen the size of a row of airplane seats.

The next day, he left for work before I awoke, and by midmorning I had made it back to the train station, ready to head to town. It was a sunny and somewhat warm March day. The train pulled in, and I got on. It was about ten minutes into the trip when I realized that I had forgotten to take notice of the name of the station where I had started.

No matter. I looked at those unpronounceable Japanese names (even the English translations) on the train map and had narrowed it down to one of three possibilities. I jotted them down in my journal and set off on my way. Somehow or other I would figure it out.

The majority of that day ended up being quite uneventful. I knew there were two major train stations and gathering areas in the center of town, and I would do my best impression of a tourist wandering between them.

The first is called Shinjuku, and it was engraved in my memory from watching the documentary movie *Baraka* several years earlier. I remember hearing that it was the busiest train station in the world. As someone who had been gravitating toward taking things slow and easy, I wasn't sure what the appeal was.

By the end of the day, I had made it to the second station and an area called Shibuya. Whereas Shinjuku seemed to be filled with business folk rushing here, there, and everywhere, Shibuya felt like a much more vibrant place. And it all coalesced around this little dog statue named Hachiko.

I came up the escalator out of the train and was pulled like a magnet to that dog. That animal was the stuff of Japanese lore. The way the story goes is that back in the 1920s there was a professor who walked to the station every day. And each evening the dog would be waiting for him at the station when he emerged so the two could walk home together.

One day at work, the man suffered a cerebral hemorrhage and died. The dog waited and waited for the man who never showed up. He would return to the station each night when the man's train was due to arrive. He did this for nine years, nine months, and fifteen days, until one day he passed on as well. It sounds somewhat sad, but it's the perfect story for a culture that values loyalty, family, and togetherness.

On this particular night, the sight of the dog was anything but melancholy. It was a Wednesday evening party. There were a few thousand people just hanging out on this unusually warm March evening. A group of drummers playing on some benches close to the statue intrigued me.

I had long dreamed of learning how to play the djembe (African drum). About six months earlier, I had purchased one whose surface was about the size of my hand. It had mostly sat by itself until that moment, but I carried it all the way to Japan and even had it clipped to my backpack that very night. Once in a while I would tap it, but that night seemed as good a time as any to learn how to play.

Not far from where these young Japanese folks were jamming away on their drums sat a man, probably in his late 50s. He caught my eye, likely because a small group of much younger foreign women sort of hung off of him. It was surreal and clear that he was the ring leader.

He noticed me and in perfect English asked me if my tiny drum and I would like to sit in with the group. At first, I resisted due to my total lack of skill or knowhow, but his patient persistence won me over. So, for the next hour I took my spot next to the drummers and wailed away on that thing. And I was transported, totally lost in an ocean of sound and time. Once in a while, I would come up for air and notice how much sound my numb hands were producing next to the symphony coming from my right.

As playtime came to an end, my fingers all abuzz, the man sat down beside me and asked me if I wanted to learn how to play. He showed me a rhythm and said if I could learn that, then I could play pretty much anything.

Well, I sat with this simple beat for a few minutes, doing my best to let it sink in. But in my slow and steady approach, it took about two more weeks of practice before it really resonated. And with it came this life-long gift.

The jam session, on the other hand, had to come to an end. The time was creeping on 11:00 p.m. It was time to go. But I had no idea where I was heading. Luckily, the trains just kept coming in succession. The first one arrived in an instant and so did the second. The third transfer, which was going to take me to my mystery station on the outskirts of Tokyo, was just waiting there, ready to take the last passengers of the night.

While I couldn't remember exactly which station I was going to, I knew it was roughly fifteen stops away. So, you can imagine my surprise when the train came into the fifth station and the announcement came over the loudspeaker that this was the end of the line.

I had no choice but to get off at that point. I found the stationmaster and pleaded my case. Although he spoke no English, it became clear that late at night this was indeed the end of the line. He even managed to find an English map of the train system and handed it to me. The only way to make it back would be to walk along the train's path. I mean, how long could it take to go ten stations?

I asked the stationmaster that very question, and with a straight face he told me it would take about four hours. And with that—like out of a movie—he disappeared. A gate came down locking the station, and I was all alone.

It was twelve thirty in the morning and time to regroup. My eye was drawn to the Circle K convenience store, and I realized how hungry I was. Those stores are essentially an homage to quick stop sushi and ramen noodles. There were tons of options, a microwave, and a collection of spices to help turn that fast-food bowl into a delicacy. Those hot and spicy noodles were like an elixir going down, and I could feel my second wind taking hold. Feeling so much better, it was time to take stock of my options.

A taxi for this penny-pinching backpacker was a nonstarter. They have a fascinating taxi culture in Japan, and I can only imagine how much ride-sharing has revolutionized that industry. Back then, the drivers all wore a formal black uniform punctuated with white gloves. They pressed a button by their side that opened and closed the back door of the cab. The meter started at $10 (1000 yen) and would stay that way for several minutes. But once it started moving, it was like a race to see how high it could climb. That four-hour walk, divided by six, carry the five, would easily cost at least $150-$200.

My next option, and perhaps the one I was most reluctant to carry through, would be to "borrow" a bike. In our small town, bikes were borrowed all the time. If you came out to find that yours was taken, chances were there would be another one in the vicinity to help pay it forward. That was why most people rode what were called *gomi* bikes, which I came to understand translated as garbage bikes. Nothing fancy, heavy steel, three speeds with a handy basket on the front.

There were literally hundreds of them parked at this station. My idea was that I would take one for the night and bike it back early the next morning. It turned out that there was one big difference between a town of 12,000 and a city of 12 million, and that was here they actually locked their bikes.

I tried every single one and each was locked except for the very last bike. There was one issue, though. This bike was missing its seat. Yet what could I do? I started riding it out of the parking lot and—I kid you not—the bike essentially fell apart in my hands. I was left holding the handles, and that was about all. It became abundantly clear I would not be borrowing a bike on this night.

That brought me to my final bright idea. As my mother is fond of saying, it was time to use Bus 11—a reference to my legs—and start walking. There was just one little twist; I was also open to hitchhiking.

I had little experience with that mode of transportation. In fact, I had only ever done it twice before in my life, and both times were in the previous couple of months in the small town where I was living. This time I'd be trying it in a totally foreign place in the middle of the night. Not only that, but I wasn't entirely sure where I was going!

This time I walked about three blocks when a white sedan full of Japanese teens stopped for me. They barely spoke a word of English, and we already know how "good" my Japanese was. But I did have that little map the station master had given me. Somehow, I managed to explain to them that I didn't know exactly which station I was heading to, but I was confident it was one of three.

They agreed to take me even though it was two thirty in the morning by that point. And here was the real kicker; those stations were far enough away that they didn't know where they were either. These were before the days of Google Maps. Cell phones were still a fairly foreign object, even in this land of technological superiority.

On that drive, I learned that even when you cannot speak each other's language, you sure can find a lot to talk about. I remember laughter and a whole lot of ease as we tried to learn a few things about each other. And all the while I was trying to convey that I was pretty sure it was going to be the first station we were driving to, but even if it wasn't, it was okay. I would get out and walk the last part.

You can imagine my horror when we arrived at that first station and I got it wrong—especially because they refused to let me leave. My embarrassment only grew when we got to the second station I was 99.9% certain had to be the one. Except it wasn't, and again they insisted on seeing this through.

At least and at last the third time was indeed the magic number. It was 4:00 a.m. and my new friends had brought me home.

Home. An important word in this story. Yes, they brought me to Yoshitada's. Just as important is the lesson they taught me, a lesson that took a whole lot longer than that djembe rhythm to really sink in.

It is the story of second impressions and one that was offered again and again in my nine-month immersion in Japan. In a word, it was generosity. The generosity of spirit, the "how can I help?" and "how can I be of service?" with no goals and no reward. Just the purest sense of giving I had ever been part of occurred time and time again.

It was followed up with the truth that...

> **Communication from the heart in many ways is way more real than the spoken word.**

And when you combine that with a deep-found respect for all beings in all forms, and include a heaping helping of human kindness to all that you do, then you're really onto something.

In this way, these new friends really did lead me Home. The spark became a flame through my relationship with Shoda-San who, perhaps more than anyone, taught me the fundamental truth of what traveling was all about (at least for me). And then I encountered it in so many surprising ways. Home is everywhere—in everyone you meet, in every leaf, and everything you come into contact with—and it's just waiting to be found.

I still ask myself, what compelled those teens to drive me, a total stranger, to the ends of the earth in the middle of the night? Why see that through to the very end? And what happens when you don't have the funds, the time, or the inclination to travel the globe to learn about the magic of Home? How else can one learn that universally important lesson?

I am reminded that this way of seeing—that I was a stranger to them—is in some ways an illusion, just part of the way I've been conditioned to see the world. And how different this would feel when embracing a different truth, the part that comes when knowing Home is everywhere and we are all one.

CHAPTER 5

My Shame & Vulnerability

Sell your cleverness and purchase bewilderment.

~Rumi

I have come to believe that each of us has a blind spot. I know I do. By that I mean an aspect of my reality where, no matter how much I work on myself to become more aware and healthy, my ego pretty much has free rein. I've ended up sabotaging my progress more times than I can count and am left scratching my head wondering why.

I can't say this for certain, but I do see it to be true among people who are closest to me, as well as for myself. For some reason, the blind spot that stands out most among those I know is pride. For me, however, it is more in numbers, in counting, which in turn leads to calculating.

When you (or I) calculate, whether we realize it or not, we end up doing things in a way that at its root continually asks, "What's in it for me?" That is how my fear tends to control my thoughts and therefore my actions. It's a deep-seated fear that connects to my self-confidence to live life to its fullest, of my own sense of self-worth and self-love. I count when I fear that I will not be supported by other people and by life itself.

Many times I've carried energy and have made choices in situations where I only gave enough to ensure a good return, to save face, to look good. I'd be scared of running out of money, of being taken advantage of, or that my contributions won't be recognized.

Whether that be in counting tips, contributing to groceries, buying a friend or a boss lunch, how much to pay an employee, you name it. That counting impulse has been with me my whole life. And when my ego gets its hands on it, it casually convinces me to calculate.

Without realizing it, this impulse has cost me dearly. It's cost me friends, jobs, and connections that I valued dearly.

> **Essentially, that fear of not being well supported becomes a self-fulfilling prophecy.**

I believed in my kindness, that I was giving enough of myself. But I was mistaken. I have long seen that principle of abundance working for me, whether that is getting the next teaching job right when I need it, getting help from strangers, and so on. Yet something within me has also convinced me of the scarcity principle and the need to protect myself, lest I run out of whatever it is that I need.

It is one thing to know that this impulse is holding me back; it is quite another to work on undoing that hold, and those deeply ingrained patterns. That is a huge part of my life work and will be for the rest of my days.

At the same time, my calculating ways are not the only things that hold me back. I have a stubborn streak which often helps but sometimes hurts. I get angry, I get hurt, and all that affects my ability to express myself.

What's more is that I have long had difficulties with communication and establishing boundaries. I can remember my mother telling me, "You're just like your father." And when she said it like that, it certainly wasn't meant as a compliment. It was intended to sting, to get the message across that I hold things too close to my chest. I don't let people in, I don't communicate enough until I end up exploding.

Now my mother and I have a very special—and profound—relationship, and we have produced our fair share of explosive "conversations." In fact, that's probably happened about forty-nine times more with her than with anyone else in my life combined. That is the perspective from which she's gotten to know me, but she does have a point.

My name is Shai, after all, and I have long been on the quieter side. Observing, observing, observing. Listening and then sometimes sharing and deciding how much is enough.

I have certainly received feedback in my intimate relationships suggesting that I do not share enough and have long been confused by those words when I feel that I have been. At the same time, I listen, I take it to heart, and ask myself where and how can I improve? Communication is, after all, the key to every healthy relationship.

After receiving this message enough times, I learned that open communication—knowing what and when to share—is something that does not come naturally to me. It's something I need to work on every single day.

Perhaps one of the reasons communication has been such a struggle is because I did not realize the value of showing vulnerability and shame. I owe a great debt to teachers like Brene Brown who teach exactly that. She shares that only by getting messy, by opening up and leaning into my vulnerabilities instead of supposedly protecting myself and others from them, do I get to experience the full range of the best that humanity has to offer.

The fact is that the opposite is true. If I don't share out of fear of hurting someone or fear of what it might do to our relationship or friendship, then I may not realize it, but I am hurting that connection even more in the long-term, and I am cutting myself off.

Another thing that I never understood well—and continue to work on—is why and how to set boundaries. I have yielded in too many situations because I like to help. I like to be of service. I have a lot to give and gravitate toward helping people in need. Maybe when combined with some of those calculating ways, I have resisted being generous with my money, but I could make up for it by giving of my efforts.

It took me a long time to realize that having limits, knowing those edges and working within them, is important both to me and those I'd like to help. When you set boundaries, and can express them in a positive way, you have more to give of yourself, and you give from a much better place. You work with the flow of things and not against the current.

So why am I sharing all these details? Because to me these are the guts, the dirty areas of my story that are part of the reason I chose to bring Spirit into my life.

I didn't, and in many ways I still don't, know how to get out of these dead ends on my own. When I find myself in that place, I ask for help and guidance away from fear, from impulses that keep me trapped. I ask for help to tap into some part of myself that I seem incapable of accessing, but which I would give anything to reach.

As my journey through my twenties and thirties went, there remained that life-long question still beating in the background. What do I want to be when I grow up? That was the case even when I was well into my Thai Massage career. For many years, I simply couldn't tell when or how I was being guided and, for a long time, I felt stuck on what to do next with my life.

Would I continue to teach or will this be a stepping stone to something else? Will I stay in the position I was in when first learning the ropes, supporting someone else's vision, or would I go out on my own and start my own school? I felt stuck because I valued listening to my gut or intuition before making these kinds of big decisions, and for many years it was as though that voice had fallen silent.

I don't think it ever left me at all. It's that through my own choices I had inadvertently cut myself off from that voice. My blind spot was no longer just a spot. It was filling up the whole framework of my perception.

In my case, eventually I did find my way through, and it did not come like a bolt of lightning. Instead it was part of a gradual change that eventually took over. One that was so slow, I didn't even realize it was happening.

Yet even through those many years of feeling frozen, I did not lose faith—at least not for long. I held onto the message that I am connected to something bigger, and it may take time, but eventually things will make more sense. I also remained convinced that love would show me the way.

One of the primary tools I used to put those ideas into practice was and is Thai Massage. Massaging has been a friend and companion on the road of life—the extent of which is hard to put into words. This is because it is hard to convey what giving from a place of comfort and connection really feels like without tasting it for yourself.

Compassionate touch has the ability to break down walls or lift the veil that keeps us separated from another person, that keeps me feeling small and in that calculating mode. It is a revelation to put hands or forearm or elbow on body and to engage in a deep exercise of listening. It is glorious to sense or be told what the body prefers and then to respond by delivering that in the best way I know how. Then, when I do engage in that moment-to-moment exercise in awareness throughout a massage, there is a cumulative effect in what I have created. I may not be conscious of it all the way through a session, but I am by the end.

In those final few moments you start slowing down. You are no longer moving about the body, you get to sit by the hands, or the head, and feel how much more sensitive you are than when you first began. What you get to experience is a merging. A bond has formed between you and your partner that is unshakeable. It feels as good as anything you can experience in life. It brings clarity of what it means to be connected. Not in theory, but in practice. To mold, to flow, to breathe, to share. That theory I've read about so many times, that we are all one, is living and breathing in every cell of my body. I feel it coursing through my veins, in my breath, in what I am able to sense in this person, and so do they. We have come together. Even if this aspect of reality were already true, now I know. That second kind of joy of which I talked about at the start of this book, which bubbles up from a deep and loving place takes over. It infuses us both with vitality, happiness, and peace.

My promise to you is that when you are feeling stuck, those glimpses and experiences act as very powerful medicine through which to keep going, to gain strength, and to nourish yourself. These are the benefits of giving that can only come with time well spent. On many a lonely day, where I didn't know whether I was coming or going, at least I had massage.

That kind of potency is only amplified when the people you massage, touch, and exchange with are at home, between lovers, family, or friends, and are those you care about and want to help. When love and appreciation already exists between you and your recipient, you have an established platform from which to grow and explore.

When those people become the focal point of giving, then you get to work on communication, the backbone of your relationship. It becomes stronger than ever because one of the secrets to giving a great massage is to honor your recipient as your primary teacher. In that way, you will put them at the center of giving. You can ask questions and ask them to teach you everything you need to know about giving an incredible massage. It is powerful stuff, and I have seen many a couple get on the mat and have dramatic breakthroughs in their relationships because of how they learn to communicate about the massage from a friendly and supportive place.

Seeing these kinds of immediate, tangible results, whether they be easing your loved one's tension, changing the whole complexion of their day, or helping someone in pain, is powerful beyond measure. You gain strength from those results, and it helps you release your own stress and whatever holds you back. Working within your means, massaging in a way that listens to your body, will also help you to feel healthier and stronger.

Finding someone, or a group of close friends and family members to exchange with regularly, gives each of you the benefits of giving and receiving. Let's not forget that receiving is amazing as well. Lying there or being moved, floating through time and space while another person puts all their compassion into you. Having your knots undone, your stress melt, your pains recede, your energy lift, and that sense of feeling better as your body heals itself, has the power to transform your mood and your energy in the moment and beyond.

Now that you are getting a deeper look at some of the unspoken benefits of giving, can you imagine how good it is to find and bring compassionate touch into your life?

How will it affect your relationships, your health, your mind, and spirit to exchange massage weekly? How will those benefits grow exponentially?

CHAPTER 6

THE SCIENCE OF TOUCH

"Spirituality isn't about manifesting what you want, it's about manifesting what you are."

~WAYNE DYER, *I CAN SEE CLEARLY NOW*

What makes giving massage that missing link on the spiritual path? How does compassionate touch bring us closer to God, spirit, one another, or however you identify with Love? Why does the very act of touching break down boundaries, give us more understanding of ourselves, align with spirit and with those we care about?

Because we are already experts in touch. We have a relationship with that sense that is as old as our first breath.

I am very fortunate in many ways. I have a daughter that I get to love more than life itself. And the timing of her coming into this world means that I was already ten or so years into my career as a massage teacher and practitioner. It was an incredible gift to see what life is like at the very beginning. To see how she made sense of the world in those first few hours, days, and months.

The role that touch played in all of that growing was immediately clear. It is the dominant sense at the start of life, and we would be lost without it. Nowadays, common practice dictates that a baby is put her on her mother's body—skin-to-skin—when she is born, so she knows she's in a safe and protected place.

I remember the first time my daughter noticed her thumb and that there was a space between her face and her digits. The way to bridge that gap was to bring her hand to her face. And that, to her, was one of her first revelations, one of her first smiles. It is no accident that in those first couple of years everything is a journey, from first touching something to picking an object up to putting it into the mouth to confirm its reality.

> **By the time we are two years old, we are all experts in touch because we've been using this sense to understand everything.**

We've been using it to create a relationship with the present moment, with our loved ones, and the world that surrounds us. By the time we reach adolescence, most of us may have forgotten its value and power, but that doesn't mean that knowledge has gone anywhere. We can access it anytime we want.

Through compassionate touch, we are afforded direct access to safety, love, abundance, and connectedness. It brings us into deep communion with each other and with ourselves in the healthiest of ways. Your partner on the receiving end gets to feel their stress and pain melt while you get a direct experience of bliss.

I read an incredible article called "Feel Me: What the Science of Touch Says About Ourselves" by Adam Gopnik in the *New Yorker* magazine in May 2016. He takes us on a journey into how touch has grown in importance in the scientific world and puts us on the forefront of some of those discoveries.

One of the first things he shares comes from neuroscientist David Linden who says, "Our entire skin is a sensing, guessing, logic-seeking organ of perception, a blanket with a brain in every micro-inch."

Gopnik shares that even in the scientific community, knowledge of the richness and diversity of this sense is relatively new. He says that, "Touch is the unsung sense: the one we depend on most and talk about the least… We see our skins as hides hung around our inner life, when in so many ways they are the inner life pushed outside."

I love and resonate deeply with that truth. Our ability to find balance, to breathe deeply, to hold onto stress, to be sick, to be well, to have good days and bad, and whatever our deepest thoughts are… it is all expressed on our skin. With our inner life, our stress, our joys, our biology all available at skin level, it shows that touching that skin with love, kindness, and awareness can have dramatic effects on those being touched and those doing the touching.

One idea Linden shared that I had never considered before is comparing the lack of touch with the loss of other senses. Many may fear going deaf or blind, and the subsequent struggles that are likely to come with it. At the same time, there are countless stories of people who overcome those challenges to live full, happy, and productive lives. Stevie Wonder is blind and has made some of the most beloved music of modern times. When we lose the use of those senses, our remaining ones become heightened to compensate, but not so with touch. In fact, the whole idea of losing our sense of touch is a foreign concept. Life is not compatible with a loss of touch, and there are no national foundations for the hard-of-touch.

Yet as Gopnik muses, "One strange thing about the unsung sense is that it has no songs. Every other sense has an art to go with it: the eyes have art, the ears have music, the nose and the tongue have perfume and gastronomy, but we don't train our hands to touch as we train our ears to listen."

I read that, and I have to laugh. Training in compassionate touch is exactly this. It is about turning touch into an art form. Combining touch with meditation, a dedication to loving kindness, a willful expression of compassion, and a wish to help one another is the art of touch. It does not live in a museum, and it is not just available and controlled by the few. It is folk art. The art of the people, by the people, for the people, and accessible to one and all.

Reaching people equals touching people: to touch is to feel.

Dacher Keltner is a psychology professor at Berkeley and the scientific adviser on Pixar's movie, *Inside Out*. In the same article, he goes on to say that, "Touch is the first system to come online and the foundations of human relationships are all touch. Skin-to-skin, parent to child, touch is the social language of our social life. It lays a basis for embodiment in feeling."

That doesn't stop as infants. It is true throughout our lives, even if we don't realize it. Imagine how much more powerful that would be—how much more powerful we would be—if we did. We could more easily and readily cross the great divide of relationships, empathy, communication, being understood, and being heard.

There's a reason there is such a cross-over between touch and our deepest feelings. Our language is filled with examples:

- You really touched me.
- That touched my heart.

To deny ourselves the experience, the exploration, the cultivation of touch, the awareness of what we're doing, is to deny ourselves a direct portal to our heart and those of our brothers, our sisters, our community, and our loved ones. It is keeping us from knowing ourselves to our fullest potential.

We may not realize it, but so much of thriving or lacking in relationships has to do with touch. When we want to show appreciation, we hug or shake hands. When we want to express our anger, we make a point of not making contact or expressing discomfort with another person when we do decide to touch. Sex—which certainly involves a lot of touch—is one of, if not the most intimate, ways to connect with another person. Keltner so eloquently shares the point that our relationship to touch is at the root of our common humanity. If we want to have healthy relationships with others and with ourselves, it is therefore imperative to know how to touch.

Keltner was also a coauthor of a study looking at twelve kinds of celebratory touches among pro-basketball players. Their conclusion was that players who touched one another a lot did better than those players who didn't. How simple it is to extract that wisdom into our everyday life. Our team is our friends, our families, our coworkers, our communities. We will all do better when we touch and are touched more often. And of course, it's the kind of touch that is fueled by encouragement, caring, kindness, and at its deepest core, love.

It may be easy to see how the person who receives that kind of touch benefits deeply, but less often do we think about the person giving it and how they benefit. Yet it is just as profound when you know you have crossed that great divide and that your love has been communicated and felt.

Quite possibly the highest evolution of the exchange that elevates touch into an art form is compassionate touch (or massage). It is rich beyond belief.

To skillfully touch and please every inch of that brain which covers us from head to toe. To engage in every part of our body to help accomplish that goal. To continually learn and grow into this mode of expression with its infinite ways of being on the giving and receiving ends of what it means to feel good. Or as Keltner helps to remind us: "Touch lowers stress, builds morale, and produces triumphs."

Imagine how much better it could be if we were to pay attention to this incredible sense. When we breathe mindfully and focus on how we touch, we connect our mind, body, heart, and feelings. We wake up to the very fabric of creation and to the experience of alive-ness bubbling up in every present moment, call it whatever you will: to Spirit, God, or Love.

That is how we turn touch into an art, and that is what speaks to the true value of giving massage, not to mention receiving it with appreciation. The good news becomes even better news when we realize and accept that, since we are already experts in touch, it is not much of a leap to become an expert in massage or compassionate loving touch.

All the tools we need are readily available in the comfort of our living rooms, and it is certainly as good a place as any to get started.

CHAPTER 7

SHIFTING FROM THE HEAD TO THE HEART

"Love is the capacity to take care, to protect, to nourish. If you are not capable of generating that kind of energy toward yourself. It is very difficult to take care of another person. In the Buddhist teaching, it's clear that to love oneself is the foundation of the love of other people. Love is a practice. Love is truly a practice."

~THICH NHAT HANH

One of the most popular—and powerful—TED talks of all time is by Jill Bolte Taylor. It's called "My Stroke of Insight." She was a Harvard brain scientist and researcher on the day she suffered a stroke on the left side of her brain. As such, she had an incredible perspective from which to observe what was happening as her left brain gradually shut down. While the stroke was happening, she got to live life almost entirely from right-brain awareness.

Our left brain is our organizing brain. It is where the *I* lives from which our identity, our roles, our sense of self as an individual is born. The *I* that says I am Shai Plonski, massage teacher, father, brother, son. It is where memories and the past live. It is also where ideas of a future are planted as we direct ourselves to be the best versions of ourselves. It is where the chattering "monkey mind" lives. Judging, questioning, analyzing, worrying, planning, you name it.

The right brain is hard-wired into our present moment and learns through our body's movements. It is making sense of the here and now. It is a world of connectedness and expansiveness. It is where inspiration and creativity and experiences of love and compassion are born.

The two parts of our brain are connected through the corpus callosum. However, since the two halves process information differently, they are completely separate from one another. They have diverse interests and are focused on entirely separate realities.

When Taylor's left brain shut down, right-brain awareness is where she went, fully and completely. To a place she lovingly calls "La La Land." She also said, following that shift, it was as if forty years of stress and emotional baggage were all of a sudden removed.

She describes it as living with the truth that, "I am an energy-being connected to the energy all around me through the consciousness of my right hemisphere. We are energy-beings connected to one another through the consciousness of our right hemispheres as one human family. And right here, right now, we are brothers and sisters on this planet, here to make the world a better place. And in this moment, we are perfect, we are whole, and we are beautiful."

Taylor finished her talk by asking the fundamental question of "Who are we?" To which she answers, "We are the life-force power of the universe, with manual dexterity and two cognitive minds. And we have the power to choose, moment by moment, who and how we want to be in the world. Right here, right now, I can step into the consciousness of my right hemisphere, where we are. I am the life-force power of the universe. I am the life-force power of the fifty trillion beautiful molecular geniuses that make up my form, at one with all that is.

"Or, I can choose to step into the consciousness of my left hemisphere, where I become a single individual, a solid. Separate from the flow, separate from you. I am Dr. Jill Bolte Taylor: intellectual, neuroanatomist. These are the "we" inside of me. Which would you choose? Which do you choose? And when?

"I believe that the more time we spend choosing to run the deep inner-peace circuitry of our right hemispheres, the more peace we will project into the world, and the more peaceful our planet will be."

I cry tears of joy every time I hear that talk. She speaks directly to the beauty of alive-ness and living a life of the highest quality, which is available to us in any given moment. We just have to be able to access our right brain. I think Taylor and I—and just about everyone else—would also agree that we don't have to have a stroke in order to access that part of our brain.

At the same time, accessing our right brain is a learned skill. It is not as simple as snapping our fingers or saying, "Okay, right brain, I'm ready for you now!" The difficulty comes because most of us have been trained and conditioned to prioritize and use our left brain. Since the two sides operate differently, we need entirely different tools and skills to access the right brain from those we've learned throughout our life.

One's ability to access the right brain comes down to retraining how we think and the choices we make as we go about our day. Growing up through university, I often found myself locked into my thinking mind, my left brain. I thought and thought until it was time to think some more.

Sir Ken Robinson, in another brilliant TED talk titled, "Do Schools Kill Creativity?" captured this reality perfectly when he described what it was like to be surrounded by university professors. He said that, "Typically they live in their heads… They're disembodied, you know, in a kind of literal way. They look upon their body as a form of transport for their heads."

I was doing my best to live up to that academic ideal and as such was essentially divorced from my body.

He goes on to add, "If you want real evidence of out-of-body experiences, get yourself along to a residential conference of senior academics, and pop into the discotheque on the last night. And there you will see it. Grown men and women writhing uncontrollably off the beat, waiting until it ends so they can go home and write a paper about it."

That separation and awkwardness described me to a T until I was twenty-one, when I discovered my hands. That summer I worked in an amusement park in a booth making wax molds of people's hands.

The process involved getting a person to make a shape with their hand like an "okay" or "a peace sign" or an "I Love U." I would then take their hand, put it in a bucket of ice cold water to numb it a little bit. From there I would transfer their hand to hot liquid wax and back into the water, and instantly a layer of wax would suction around the hand. By repeating the process, I added more layers until the wax hand was strong enough and then I would remove it, color it, and sometimes turn it into a candle.

Lo and behold, you had your hand! It turned out, I was a natural at it, and I got to meet and make thousands of hands that summer. Yet, to my greatest surprise, in my alone time, the hands I really got to meet intimately were my own.

Sitting alone at night on the boardwalk after a fourteen-hour work day, I could sense and feel energy in my hands. I could feel how they wanted to move almost like they had a mind all their own. In fact, they did have a mind all their own. And in getting to know my hand, I had such a tangible taste of Spirit. I shifted from my mind to my heart as expressed through my body.

From there, all bets were off. It turned out that I loved to dance, which was news to me. It turned out that by embracing what the right side has to offer, my life became richer, and my intuition became stronger. What those times signified were some of my first adult forays into seeing and living with mind and body coming together, through my right brain. I just needed to make room for it.

That doesn't mean I am putting down the left brain. The left brain is of vital importance. It is the means through which I take inspiration and make sense out of it. The problem was that the left brain had been given priority. It was how I was trained to think. I became trapped and lived a life that was very much out of balance. It also gave my ego free reign to control my thoughts and my emotions. That means a whole lot of choices were based on fear, on calculating, on protecting myself, and on cutting myself off from others.

That ego still lives and breathes in me, but now my everyday includes a conscious effort to surrender to the big *I*. That's because I know that I am so much more than the little *I*. When we love, tap into spirit, communicate and have communion with one another, this universe we call Home is a much richer place to live.

These days, I try to use my left-brain awareness to bring right-brain creativity into form. I've also learned that you can't force the right brain to reveal itself. Bringing out the right brain is an exercise in non-force. All I can do is make choices that allow for a healthy inner environment. That includes paying attention to my breath, meditating regularly, getting into nature, and practicing yoga. It also means embracing the virtue of patience. These are all parts of my personal practice. I choose to make a conscious effort to pay attention, hopefully without thoughts of success or failure. I accept that I can and do fail all the time, and then when I notice that I've become distracted, I come back to my breath and to nurturing that healthy environment.

By definition, right-brain awareness is spontaneous. It is always with us, connecting us with our environment, but for most people I know, in order for it to become present in one's awareness, we need to consciously make space for it.

That right-brain awareness comes through loud and clear when you are connecting with yourself and with others. It comes through in great conversations, sharing from the heart, and having a personal practice. It comes through when you love with an open heart without goals or expectations. It comes through when you do things you genuinely like to do and even more so in the company of people you like to spend time with. It comes through when you put that love at the center of your values and religion.

Giving massage as compassionate touch is about as great a way as any to fine-tune your awareness. It's a wonderful way to shift from the head to the heart. It puts all the benefits in your personal practice and brings them to life. Compassionate touch helps you share the best of yourself with another person. It aids in transcending "otherness" and that veil that says there's a separation between you and me. Instead, it shows you what life is like when you merge, become larger than the sum of your parts. To be moved by giving, by spirit, by another person, and the wonder of it all.

> **Giving massage from a place of comfort and caring is the antithesis of stress and the patterns that might have caused so many of those issues to begin with.**

Compassionate touch has also been a way to show I care when I cannot find the words. That can be especially true when massaging family members. Sometimes it might be massaging someone I'm angry with or who is frustrated with me or with whom I feel blocked in knowing what to say in difficult or tender moments. This kind of touch gives me a completely different way to relate, and very often that can spark the creativity and the words needed to mend fences, get closer, and become more appreciative of one another.

Giving compassionate touch is a way to help someone you care about while also helping yourself. That helping of yourself is not just lip service. Massage helps you on every level. You get physically stronger from giving, you grow more confident in your abilities from helping others, you improve your ability to communicate, you explore nonsexual intimacy, and break down barriers borne of fear. You get more comfortable in your body, with your body, and with another person's body. You share spaces of reverence with your partner, with yourself, and with Spirit. Those moments of stillness and touch will be alive with life and the knowledge that you are part of something more. When you give compassionate touch in this way, you experience the right brain so bright and so clear. You become aware of what it means to be connected and how meaningful it is.

As you continue to give massage regularly, especially with the same person over an extended period of time, all of these benefits increase exponentially. You are not the same person as when you started; you transform just as a caterpillar turns into a butterfly.

The massage becomes part of your spiritual practice, and it is grounded in your relationships. This brings tremendous feelings of gratitude as your heart becomes lighter and you become freer. Compassionate touch becomes a friend for life, a friend you can access whenever you want and certainly through times of need.

I have endured tremendous loss in my life: the end of a relationship, the loss of a loved one, and the loneliness that I sometimes feel on any given day and without warning. Massaging on those days are often the most challenging experiences, until you get on the mat or the bed or table.

It takes about two painstaking minutes of giving to get over the hump, and then you start to melt so that "You" can take over. Whatever it was that had you feeling down has been transformed into something that is so different.

That hardship you were feeling doesn't magically disappear every time, but by the time you're done, you have changed, and you often feel so much more able to find your way.

You have truly tapped into the joy of giving, the joy of living and of connecting from a place of authenticity. It is real and beautiful, and it fills you up with the experience of feeling so good and so healthy. What a gift you get to give yourself while touching those you care about.

This is what giving can mean, why it is a missing link in one's personal practice, and how it can enrich relationships. It is in this way that I encourage you to learn and to practice. It's as if you're about to step into one of life's great adventures. You have it in you. It lives right there at the tip of your fingers and the point of your elbows. It is life brimming inside you, experienced in all its glory, that you get to share with another person.

My daughter got to know the space between her hands and face and the rapture of connecting that distance within the first couple weeks of life. Perhaps I had the same experience when I was her age, but from what I can remember, I was also about twenty-one years late to the party. Whatever age you are, I can assure you that it is never too late, and the music is still going strong.

As you prepare to learn the practice, keep in mind that giving massage is about to become one of the great journeys and joys of your life.

PART II

LEARNING COMPASSIONATE TOUCH

⌘

"My body told me it had a friend called mind. My mind whispered sweet nothings about a body. And my heart yearned for an experience to help me stay connected and wake up from any illusion of separateness."

~ALEXIS MULHAUSER

CHAPTER 8

LEARNING AT HOME

Have you ever seen the animated film *Ratatouille*? It is all about a rat named Remy living in France. He loves fine foods and is unwilling to eat the same kind of leftovers enjoyed by his rat family. One day, at the human house where he lives, Remy sees a gourmet chef on the TV promoting his new cookbook which has, at its core, the idea that anyone can cook.

Remy, enamored by that principle, decides to leave the house to follow his dream. He will go to Paris so he can become a great chef. The greater lesson in the movie is not necessarily that everyone can cook, but that anyone can become great.

When it comes to giving a truly incredible massage, I humbly believe that anyone *can* cook. In Part One, we discovered that we are already experts in touch.

What we are also experts at is metta. Metta means loving kindness and compassion. It is not just romantic love, although that could certainly fall under its umbrella. It is the love we have for humankind, for nature, for the universe. It is the energy of the present moment and a core experience of right-brain awareness. It is the creative force behind the question, "How can I help?"

And even if you count yourself among the population that doesn't experience these feelings and sensations all that often, you are still an expert in metta. I know this because you are reading this book. You are alive. The only way you could be alive is because your body engages in metta-filled energy and choices trillions of times a day.

Your heart pumps blood to every cell in your body. It doesn't say, "Foot, you did a bad job yesterday, so I'm going to hold back." It is automatic and without question. You want to learn something new? Then every part of your body that's needed jumps into the fray. If you injure your right leg, your left leg is not going to say, "Good luck with that." It says, "How can I be of service?" And it, along with your back, your shoulders, your neck, and a trillion other cells, take on the extra work to give the injured part a hand.

You may not realize it, but these are choices that our body makes, and we are making them in our favor and in the spirit of metta all the time, in more ways than we could ever realize.

> **Metta is the most important, and perhaps the only ingredient you need to give that incredible experience of compassionate touch.**

Everything else is a tool to bring that energy to life and into ever greater expression. And in learning how to give that compassionate touch, you have many tools at your disposal in your own home.

Giving massage, Thai Massage, compassionate touch, or whatever you want to call it, is democratic. Anyone can learn enough moves to give a great twenty-, thirty-, or even sixty-minute treatment with the right coach and approach. But as *Ratatouille* reminds us, for that greatness to come, you need to be willing to try. Learning this skill, like any new thing you want to undertake, is not automatic.

There are great powers at work within us that make learning anything new a huge challenge, and those are our subconscious habits. Knowing about this internal wiring helps you so that instead of fighting against the current, you go with the flow.

While learning this skill, along with anything else, you will no doubt experience a phase of pure excitement and joy. It's as though your adrenaline takes over and you feel like you can move mountains. But at some point, a different law of the universe—inertia—takes over. It sneaks up on you and, if you're not careful, this new passion dwindles out and you revert back to previous habits.

There is a biological reason for this, but to affect lasting change you must plan for that pattern to try to influence you. You should accept that at some point your mind is going to try to revert back, and you should know what you're going to do to overcome it.

And this is one way the left-brain comes in to support your right-brain enthusiasm. When you make your learning plan, keep in mind that according to experts I've learned from—along with personal experience—it generally takes thirty days for a new habit to become permanent. As such, prepare to be extra vigilant and dedicated in these first thirty days. Ask yourself honestly where and how you can commit to learning and then practicing.

There are many ways to learn and practice, and they do not always require having a partner. That is no doubt the most fun and should be part of the goal. But it's far from the only way to get in the zone and, right now in these first thirty days, you need to get in the zone consistently. Which is why I'm asking you to make a thirty-day practice plan and consider your choices.

Here are some of the other ways you can practice besides exchanging with a partner.

- Reread this book
- Take notes
- Watch the accompanying videos
- Visualize yourself massaging someone you care about
- Do a shadow dance

That last option is akin to Tai Chi; it's a slow self-practice. Visualize the person you want to massage, get your massage space and equipment ready, and literally go through the massage, practicing your transitions and moves.

When I was first learning, the most valuable method was to visualize giving. I would lie in bed at the end of the day and see myself back in the massage space giving what I had learned. The key was to visualize myself clearly in action in whatever pose I was having difficulty with. If my brain skipped a pose or I got distracted, I would simply rewind the massage in my head to the last place I remembered.

Then, the next time I had a chance to practice on someone, it was incredible to see how well that exercise helped. Understanding the power of the mind in your training is an important thing to know about the learning process.

Perhaps you've seen videos of tennis players or skiers doing something similar. They will hold the racket and see the game they are about to play or the turns on the hill. Our body has the amazing ability to process that hill or that game or that massage as if it were the real thing. To your brain, it is as real as having that person in front of you.

What's more is that when you sleep—or when you are engaged in a different activity—your mind will continue to process and integrate the massage. That is also part of the metta energy working for you. Your brain is helping you and helping itself, so that the next time you massage a person everything feels easier.

That's what our body is designed to do. Whether you call it homeostasis or balance, your body is working toward a deeper sense of integration, toward making things easier. That process is universal, but if you improve your input with good habits, a healthy environment, good food, and so on, the better it's all going to feel.

Dan Gilbert, in his TED talk "The Surprising Science of Happiness," shares how our prefrontal cortex works to give us this uniquely human experience, and how it is one of the most valuable tools we have on the path to happiness. It is important to set the right habits from the very beginning. Mindset is key, and I know you can do it.

You can learn the massage techniques taught in this section in three hours or so. You can also divide up the material into smaller pieces and learn one or two things at a time. It would be ideal to learn this with another person and plan an afternoon or two to study and practice together. From there, going forward, schedule one day a week to give and another to receive.

How often you practice is up to you, but the key—if you want to incorporate this into your life—is to find consistency and focus. Use the tools that we've discussed and practice. Finding the people will come as long as you are making space for it in your life.

This section of the book is going to teach you everything you need to give a twenty-to-thirty-minute massage. In sharing this knowledge, I leave no stone unturned. My aim is to bring the fullness of my teaching experience so that you feel supported and able to give a truly incredible massage to anyone you like. I have been fine-tuning and using this system for over fifteen years. I have never seen anyone go through the program who is not able to give a great massage on their own. We will take it step by step, and it will become clear with each coming chapter.

CHAPTER 9

THE TOOLS OF THE TRADE

efore we get started, there are two vital parts of your support system. The first is embracing all of the teachers that help you learn how to give such a great massage. The second is the tools available.

There are multiple teachers to help you learn how to give an incredible massage. In order of importance, these are:

- Your partner(s)
- The Four Pillars of the Massage
- This book and the accompanying videos

Your Partner

> **The people you massage are hands down your most important teacher.**

It is vital to keep this in mind and heart. They are the ones who have agreed to be touched and massaged. They are the ones who are agreeing to forfeit some amount of control of their body to you.

They are the ones—through their insights into what feels good—that will help you discover the unspoken language of intuition and intent. They will be the ones who will help you feel more alive and so incredible from the experience of giving from the body, mind, and heart.

It is imperative to take that commitment at full value, to honor them as your primary teacher, and to treat their body as something sacred. When you treat your partner with this kind of reverence, then your massage becomes a practice ground for nurturing your relationships. And this kind of attention can have a big impact on the rest of your life. One of the keys to giving a great massage is the same as a great relationship, and that is outstanding communication.

I will explain some of the ways to establish that outstanding communication, but for now let's agree to engage in mindful means of sharing. Let's agree that one of the best ways to learn how to massage comes from asking your partner how they are receiving the massage. And part of our task is to coach them so that they feel safe and encouraged to tell us what they are feeling, unprompted. The more they can tell us what they like, the better equipped you will be to deliver that.

An underlying theme of how I teach is to take the mystery out of the massage. If you're not sure whether you're giving enough or too much pressure, then ask. If you're massaging an area that has a lot of tension or is the site of a previous injury, then ask how it feels.

When you give a massage, so much of what you do is a calculated risk. That's especially true when you explore someone's edges around pressure and working areas of the body that are shouting out to be touched. As such, there is no such thing as asking too often about how the massage is feeling and encouraging your partner to let you know what they are feeling.

We're not only trying to avoid injury or doing something that they may not enjoy. In fact, I can virtually guarantee that if you practice with respect for your partner and work within the system I'm teaching you, then there is no chance of injuring your partner.

Massage is all about taking something that feels really good and figuring out how to make it feel even better, and then to repeat that process again and again.

Part of honoring your partner as your number-one teacher is working with the knowledge that they know what they like. So, if you've found a great spot to massage, say for example around their left shoulder blade, and they've told you about it, then use that information to your advantage. Because odds are there's another really great spot just a few centimeters away from that first spot that'll feel just as good, if not better.

The bottom line is that the more you can identify the key spots where they like to be massaged, the better you'll be at finding even more of those great spots.

Their body is also changing from moment to moment and certainly from massage to massage. Even if you are massaging the same person every week or so, it doesn't mean that you're massaging the exact same body.

What was a major issue last week may have disappeared this week, in part because of your massage. But there may be new spots that crop up. Great communication is important to practice every day and during every massage. What's more, you will improve with every massage you give.

I've come to learn that memory is selective. When you're helping your partner to feel really great, that is what stands out from the experience. That is all he or she will remember. I don't ever recall giving a massage or getting feedback from my students that their partners complained because of too much checking in during the session.

Learning to Receive Is a Skill

Just as giving a massage is a learned skill, so is learning to receive. There may certainly be some people who lie down for a massage with the energy and attitude of "do what you want with me," but that's not always going to be the case.

Many people agree to receive a massage but still need help with letting go and relaxing. Think about it, if you spend most of your day seemingly in control of your life and body, what we are asking in a massage is a big departure from that mindset. And the challenge could be that much greater if the person on the receiving end is in pain, nursing an injury, or going through a stressful period.

First, accept that learning how to receive is just as much a skill as learning to give. Therefore, your patience is important. The key to helping your partner learn to receive is through great communication. The more you talk to them, the more they will be reassured that you are there to help. They will understand that you are only interested in doing things that feel good. If you do accidentally do something wrong, like apply too much pressure in a move or go too quickly into a spot or a stretch, if there's already been great communication between you and the recipient, it will not be the end of the world. They will likely accept that it was an accident and be more than willing to keep on relaxing into the massage.

Just as in any relationship, there is a power dynamic at play when you massage. And as the giver you need to embrace the fact that the ultimate power remains with the receiver. It is their body, and they have agreed to be touched and massaged by you. Our commitment is to do that to the best of our ability, to honor that sacred space, and to remember that they are in charge. And if ever they want to end the massage, you'll agree to that as well. It could even be a great idea to communicate that idea before you start.

Let them know that they are in charge, that you value their feedback, and that it will help you to learn how to give them the best massage possible. And if the massage ever feels uncomfortable or if they'd like you to stop, then they just need to ask.

The Four Pillars

There are four pillars or building blocks to every massage move and transition. These are the foundation of your physical practice. The same way that complex structures are built with simple shapes, a great massage is built on these four pillars. When you know these four pillars, you can give just about any massage move. You could open a book or turn on a video and be able to figure out how to do it and to do it in a way that honors these pillars.

We will go into the pillars in depth in the following chapters, but for now let's state them and start committing them to memory.
1. Meditation and Metta—two sides of the same coin of mindfulness.
2. Stances—the ways you position and use your body when you massage.
3. Rocking—the movement of your body to help massage.
4. Touch—all the ways you massage your partner.

When it comes to learning the techniques, these four pillars are your teacher. They will give you the confidence to know what you're doing and how to adjust if something doesn't feel ideal. They are the core of the practice, and they have been my teacher ever since I began.

Even when you learn in a classroom, there are only so many hours and days that you'll be in the presence of a teacher. Most learning happens when you go home. As such, the four pillars, in combination with your partner, are your primary teachers.

You're Not Alone

I am more of a facilitator than a teacher. My style is to help you discover that fundamentally the best learning happens when you embrace that you are both the student and the teacher. It is you that teaches yourself when you are in class, and you who will teach yourself when you're at home.

Having people to massage, in combination with applying the Four Pillars, are the key ways you become your own teacher. My job is to support with this book, with the techniques offered, along with the resources at your fingertips that help you embrace your inner teacher.

My role is to support your learning and to use all the tools I have to aid in your development. Learning and teaching are fluid as new ideas and better technologies come into play. I am open to all of those methods. What's more, I embrace that the best way to learn and teach is with the truth that we are all one another's teachers.

CHAPTER 10

THE FIRST PILLAR: MEDITATION AND METTA

In the previous chapter, I mentioned there are four pillars that you need to learn which are part of the foundation of compassionate touch. These pillars give you strength and know-how. They help you to become your own teacher, self-reliant in how to make yourself feel good in the act of giving compassionate touch. And at the same time, they will teach you the secrets of giving an incredible massage.

If you ever learned a martial art or participated in a spelling bee or took a ballet class or tried your hand at any other number of skills, you know what these pillars are about. Essentially, they are the core of the practice. If you were to deconstruct any pose, any transition, any movement into and out of your massage, you will find these four pillars. Get to know these well and there's nothing you can't do!

Another way of looking at it is that there is just one pillar from which the rest emanate. That is the first one, meditation and metta.

Meditation and metta are two sides of the same coin of mindfulness. Meditation exists in every spiritual and religious tradition and in some form or other for every person. There are many ways to define what it means to meditate. I define it as a conscious effort to pay attention to the here and now. And in bringing ourselves into the present, we connect with Presence. Any time you get drawn into an activity, a book, or a physical exercise, it is all a form of meditation. Meditation implies creating a healthy environment to allow for inspiration, creativity, and Presence to flow into our minds, hearts, and bodies.

There are many tools and techniques to help us turn inward. A candle, a focal point, eyes open, eyes closed, and so on. I have long worked with the breath as my focal point. This is because my breath is always with me, and it is always happening in every given moment. As such, when I can find it, I have an anchor that brings my mind into the present moment. It doesn't matter where I am, my breath comes with me.

Breath is also one of our first teachers. The miracle of life, the feeling of being alive, is contained in our ability to breathe. When you notice your breath, it is like holding up a mirror to get a deep reflection of where you are right now.

Is your breath short and labored? That is probably a sign you are experiencing stress, are distracted, ill, disconnected from your body, or some combination of all of the above. Is your breath long and fluid? Does it extend deep into your diaphragm, and are you able to notice it moving through all parts of your lungs? Then you are likely feeling centered and present.

It is your body's most essential fuel. We can only go a few minutes without oxygen, whereas we can go days without water and even longer without food. It is literally the fuel that powers every cell of your body. Each of your cells has a power station called the mitochondria, and part of its job is to convert oxygen into the energy your cells needs to function. When you pay attention to your breath, it's as though you are on a magic carpet ride. With practice and patience, you can literally get to know every part and every cell of your body.

You will not always be successful in your efforts. You'll be distracted by a thought, a phone, a beep, an idea that brings you into the past or the future. Part of a meditation practice is to accept that as par for the course. It is what you do with the next breath or moment that counts. The best you can do is recognize it when you're distracted, and with kindness, guide yourself back to your breath. If you are not capable of finding that kindness, if you are hard on yourself when you get distracted, then as soon as you can, accept that is how you are feeling.

What you are doing, breath by breath, is training yourself in the ways of the right brain. This cannot be an act of force or will. Rather it is in surrender and letting go that you shift. The act of paying attention means that you get to know yourself from the inside-out. There is an inner universe of activity and energy as complete, meaningful, and exciting as anything you experience on the outside, if not more so. A meditation practice turns your attention inward, to foster that relationship, and deepens a connection to Spirit. It also teaches you that you are not your thoughts or that chatting that seems to follow you everywhere. All you have to do to access these states of understanding and consciousness is let go of goals and expectations, bring in acceptance, and breathe! And if at first you don't succeed, simply try, try again.

There is no doubt that the more you can make meditation a regular part of your life, the better your massage, and in all likelihood your life, will be. You'll tap into sources of energy you didn't know you had. You'll learn how to let go of stress and tune into optimal feelings of health and wholeness.

It doesn't have to be more than a few minutes a day. One way is to find a comfortable seated position with your shoulders relaxed and neck long. You can sit on a cushion, on the ground, on a chair, or however you feel comfortable.

Begin by taking a few breaths. Notice your inhalation and exhalation and slowly relax into it. Feel your inhale moving in through your nostrils and up to the crown of your head. Feel your exhalations moving through you and into your body. Keep breathing into it, into you. Continue paying attention and becoming a silent witness, getting to know yourself from the inside out.

And if you feel your attention wandering, simply take notice of that and guide yourself back to your breath.

Breathe…

From there, get to know your physical body. Send your attention down to your feet. What do they feel like? Maybe it feels like tingling, tickling, warmth, or perhaps you cannot sense any sensation. If it helps, wiggle into it or simply observe no sensation. Continue to notice the rest of your leg. Shift your awareness to the other foot and leg.

Once you reach your torso, breathe into your lower body, feeling yourself like the roots of a plant, grounding into your body, and into the Earth. Keep breathing into it. Notice now your lower back, mid-back and upper back, your abdomen, lungs, and chest. Breathe into the center of your body. Breathe into your arm, your hands, and your fingers on one side and then the next.

Notice your neck and teeth, your nose, your eyes, your ears all the way up to the crown of your head and all the spaces in between.

Start breathing again into your whole body, from head to toe. Keep being a silent witness as you relax into yourself. Keep breathing into it, and send these vibrations of metta, of loving kindness and compassion and feelings of forgiveness and acceptance into every cell of your body. Now send it outward to your loved ones and to the whole universe.

At the end of a meditation, I love to say namaste. That means the wisdom that is in me bows to the wisdom that is in you.

Namaste.

If you'd like to meditate along to a free guided meditation, then check out this playlist on my YouTube page, which has all of the four pillars: **bit.ly/2tGSq0B.**

As you are engaged in this act of mindful breathing or meditating, you are likely to notice feelings of euphoria. A smile that wells up inside you, your body relaxing, warmth in your hands, good feelings in your heart, good ideas in your mind. Whatever the expression, they are all aspects of metta.

> **Metta is the energy of the present moment, and it means loving kindness and compassion.**

It is both the wish and the experience of universal love for all beings. It's that energy of "How can I help and be of service?" And it's the power of loving creativity. The more you are in touch with the present moment the more this energy is noticed and experienced throughout the day.

Even if you feel you have never experienced metta (or called it that), you already have and live with this energy in total abundance. It is simply operating on a subconscious level. Meditating helps you to notice it and bring it to your awareness. And as such, it becomes an even more powerful agent to bring positivity, change, and love into your world and the collective universe.

We are made up of thirty-seven trillion cells or more. That is a mind-numbing number! Our cells are so small and so good at doing their service that we almost never notice them (unless of course our health is compromised, then we can't help but notice them!). Each of those cells is an individual, a unit separate from the one next to it. But at the same time and by design, those cells work together for the collective good. When you want to learn something new like giving a massage and your left arm has to be engaged, it is not as if your left shoulder says, "Good luck with that!"

Everything is simply at the ready saying, "How can I help?" We certainly notice that spirit at work for us whenever we hurt ourselves. If I sprain my right ankle, my left leg takes on more of my weight so I can continue to function to the best of my ability. It may be automatic, but that doesn't mean that on some level of consciousness a choice isn't being made. The choice, again and again, is metta. It is loving kindness. It is the energy of the present moment because all of our brilliant cells can't help but be in the here and now.

Giving compassionate touch or Thai Massage is all about creating a metta massage filled with love and presence. It is a physical act of loving kindness. It is taking all that goodness that we feel in ourselves and sharing it inward while sharing it with another person and with our world.

A great friend of mine, Kaline Kelly, who is also an incredible Thai Massage teacher and practitioner, once told me the greatest massage she ever received was from an elderly woman in a small village in Thailand. What the woman did for the entire massage was to squeeze Kaline. She squeezed Kaline's arms, her legs, her shoulders, her body. This woman was so tuned into the love pouring out of her that this love was her true Self, and it had a profound healing effect.

That is why when you are present, when you practice with care and metta, then you can never go wrong. It is the only prerequisite for giving a great massage. The techniques that you choose to practice are secondary and will help channel that abundant love.

At the same time, whatever techniques you do decide to give should come from a place of mutual benefit. It should feel as good to give as it does to receive.

Get in touch with some of those thirty-seven trillion cells, with the energy of metta infusing them and infusing you. Feel yourself feeling better, feel that inner smile or, if you like, think of something or someone that helps to bring it out, and breathe. Tune into your body's inner intelligence, that knowingness of moving toward feeling good, toward inner peace, balance, and healing.

It's a wisdom that is working for and with you in every moment of every day. And as you tune in and become a silent witness, you discover that in fact you are that wisdom. As you move from left-brain awareness and into the right brain, notice that you are life, you are love, and you are connected to creativity, abundant energy, to one and all.

CHAPTER 11

THE SECOND PILLAR: STANCES

The second pillar will help you to know yourself in physical space. It is all about how to…

> **Use your whole body to give the massage.**

When giving compassionate touch, your power should never feel forced. It flows naturally. Everything you do when giving the massage should come from your core, the center of your body. You use your whole body to help every step of the way.

A stance is the body position you choose that helps you utilize your whole body. More generally, it refers to using and having good body mechanics.

A Few Guiding Principles

The first principle is to face your work. Your work is the area that you are massaging. If you are massaging someone's shoulders, then your head, your shoulders and your body should all face that direction.

The second principle is called the ABCDs of Thai Massage. Whenever possible (and I will let you know when there are exceptions to this rule) you should make sure your:

- Arms are straight, but not locked.
- Back is straight, but not stiff.
- Chin is neutral, neither looking up or down.
- Dog tail is sticking out. This is another way of saying stick your bum out, which lengthens your back and engages your core even more.
- Smile! For fun and obvious reasons, whether it's an inner or outer smile.

This massage is designed to be performed on a mat on the ground, a massage table, or on a bed. You can choose whichever is most comfortable for you and your partner. If your partner is not able to be on the ground with ease, then practice on a bed or table. If you have difficulty being on your knees or bending your knees, then you can stand or sit next to the bed. The descriptions of each technique in the massage will help you no matter which surface you choose to practice on.

If you are giving this massage on a bed or a massage table, then not all of these stances will apply to you. Most of the time you will be sitting on a chair or standing. The Warrior and Tai Chi stances will still come into play.

Keeping that in mind, here are the stances to practice for the upcoming massage.

Diamond Stance

Kneeling and sitting on your heels. Your feet can be crossed or side-by-side. Back is straight, eyes looking forward.

Variation: Sitting up on your toes while sitting on your heels.

On a bed: You won't need this stance. Instead, you'll stand at the edge of the bed or sit on a chair as needed.

Safety note: This can be a difficult stance if you are not used to sitting on your knees. When I started out, it took a few days before I could sit like this comfortably. You can adapt this pose by tucking a yoga block or pillow between your knees and bum to help take pressure off your knees and/or ankles.

Open Diamond Stance

Similar to Diamond, but with the knees separated.

Variation: You can also sit on your toes while still sitting on your heels. Come off your knees and elevate your stance to accommodate for size differences.

On a bed: You may not need this stance when giving on a bed. Instead, you can stand wide-legged.

Safety note: This stance is generally much easier to spend time in than the diamond stance. You can also tuck a pillow or yoga block between your heels and bum if needed.

Kneeling Diamond Stance

Bring the knees together and come up on your knees.

On a bed: Standing comfortably next to the bed replaces this stance.

Warrior Stance

Raise your left knee up and bring the foot flat on the floor with leg extended. Do not extend the knee beyond the toes.

Variation: Gliding warrior is used to make adjustments in distance between you and your recipient. You can move in warrior by extending your front leg and then sliding your back leg along the mat. What's important to remember is that what you do with your front leg needs an equal response from the back leg and vice versa, so that you remain balanced and strong with each movement.

On a bed: Warrior can be used on a bed depending on your balance. It can also be replaced with standing next to the bed and using Tai Chi stance.

Tai Chi Stance

Stand, keep your legs hip-width apart. Your front leg is bent while your back leg is straight and pointed at a forty-five-degree angle.

On a bed: You will use this stance when standing next to the bed. You won't need it if you're giving the massage on a mat on the floor.

CHAPTER 12

THE THIRD PILLAR: ROCKING

When was the last time you were gently rocked back and forth?

> **The rocking motion is a powerful healing movement that takes us back to a time of safety and comfort when we were young.**

When we were in the womb, we were rocked. It was a beehive of activity in there, and once we came out we were constantly rocked to help soothe our fears and tears. That is because our caregivers instinctively mimic those safe times of being in the womb.

Bringing awareness to the rocking elements of the massage is therefore a powerful component using your whole body to give, while at the same time nurturing and relaxing your partner effortlessly.

To use your whole body to give the massage, you must ensure it is moving. When it moves, your efforts are coming from your core. When it is static, chances are the part of your body making contact with your partner—such as your palms or thumbs—is doing more work than it needs to.

One of the reasons to pay attention to the third pillar of rocking is to gain all the leverage your body can offer.

Putting These First Three Pillars Together Means:

- Paying attention, which allows you to address your partner in the moment while filling up with metta.
- Choosing a stance that helps you use your whole body to massage.
- Moving with your whole body so that the effort flows from your core to your extremities.

Getting in touch with the rocking element of the massage facilitates a positive exchange of energy. Most Eastern traditions believe, and Western science has gone on to prove, that we are made up of energy. We see our bones, our skin, our muscles, and feel as though we are solid, but at a cellular level we are energy in movement. We can help to release stress, deep-seated tensions, and blockages by facilitating a positive exchange of energy. You are communicating to your partner that you are feeling good and have all this goodness within you that you are offering to them.

The energetic aspects of the massage may not mean much to you at the start. Developing a relationship to energy and the subtler aspects of giving and receiving can take time. I know it took several years before I developed a deeper sense of this aspect of massage. My suggestion is that while you give, you focus on metta. Simply give with your heart, and that is more than enough.

At the same time, know that by becoming aware of the rocking elements of the massage, you are helping facilitate that exchange of metta. You are giving it and at the same time receiving it from your partner. You are helping to connect both you and your partner to a feeling of safety and freedom on an unconscious level through the simple act of rocking.

If you've ever received a Thai Massage or watched an experienced practitioner give a treatment, then you'll have noticed a fluidity to the movements. It is a dance, and the rocking are your moves. And if you don't consider yourself a dancer, that's all right! The good news is that rocking consists of very simple movements that you can master in a few moments.

To practice these rocks, put yourself in open diamond position or sit on a chair and away you go!

Practicing the Rocking Movements

To begin your practice, find your back straight, shoulders relaxed, and neck long. Place your hands on your knees and begin to engage these two rocking movements, while paying attention to how this feels on your body.

Forward Rock

As the name implies, rock forward and then rock back. There is a slight nuance involved. When moving forward, notice how your chin moves forward and when moving backward, the chin is slightly tucked to help protect your back.

Side Rock

Sometimes I call this bamboo rock. If you've ever been to Thailand and seen bamboo, they are tall, grass-like reeds. And in the monsoon season, when the winds pick up, the reeds bend, but the base stays strong.

In side rock, you move your body from side to side while staying rooted in your base. Think of a pendulum swinging on a clock or a metronome on a piano. Your body does not collapse, it simply moves from side to side.

CHAPTER 13

The Fourth Pillar: Touch & the Secrets to Giving an Outstanding Massage

Things are about to get juicier! You have learned the first three pillars, which have been all about you—the giver—and getting to know yourself in the physical space of massaging. Now you are ready to focus on how to share compassionate touch with your partner.

This last pillar is all about touch, how to nurture the quality of touch, and explore the different parts of your body you use to touch. This is what I consider to be *the* secret to giving an outstanding massage.

In the beginning, I relied on my partners, friends, and family to teach me what it meant to give them a good massage. That is also your beginning point, so it is important to have reverence and respect for this relationship and for the fact that your loved ones are trusting you with their bodies. You do this with the secret to giving an incredible massage. In one sentence it all boils down to: "How slow can you go; how high can you fly?"

What that means is…

> **The more gradual you are, the more you can ease into what you are doing, the better your massage is going to be.**

At the introduction to the four pillars, I mentioned that one way to understand the pillars was as one pillar, meditation and metta, from which the other pillars flow.

The stances and the rocking are insights that help bring meditative awareness to your body. How slow can you go, how high can you fly will help you bring that same awareness, establish a meaningful connection, and develop the quality of touch between you and your partner.

You want to ease into what you are doing because it will help you to develop a highly refined quality of touch. This approach will help you become more sensitive and aware of all of the nonverbal cues your partner is giving about what feels good and how to increase those feelings of letting go and relaxation. If you want to become attuned to your partner, it requires paying attention with the understanding and attitude that, as much as you know, there is always more to learn about how to help and be of service. Having a slow and steady approach helps you in all facets of giving and learning those subtle qualities.

At the same time, how slow can you go puts your partner at ease. If they feel you taking your time (and we'll define more of what that means in a moment) then they will instinctively relax more easily into the massage. For many people, receiving massage is a skill just the same way giving is. Just because someone has agreed to receive your touch does not mean that they know how to give up control of their body. That is especially true if they are not used to it or you, or if they have a hard time ceding control in other parts of their life.

I have often thought of receivers on a spectrum. At one end are people who show up, lie down and say, "Do with me what you will." At the other are those who agreed to be touched and aren't sure why because they don't really like massages. Most people will be somewhere in the middle. And no matter where people are at the start, their body is designed to protect itself. If their body feels something it doesn't like, is uncomfortable, or feels pain, then it will tense up. That is part of the body's natural defense system. By easing into the massage, you help prevent that self-defense mechanism from ever coming to the forefront.

While you're going slow, make sure to also practice outstanding communication.

In this massage, we want to encourage dialogue. We want to take the mystery out of the massage. Take away the expectation that somehow, mystically, you will just know what to do and how to touch your partner in some magical way. Instead, I want to encourage you to accept that when giving massage you are taking many calculated risks.

Anytime you give pressure close to what may be your partner's maximum comfort level, anytime you massage an area of tension, anytime you massage an area that was injured, there is some risk involved that what you're doing will hurt. The way to reduce or eliminate those risks is to talk while you're easing in and paying great attention. Ask how it's feeling and ask for guidance as you start massaging a tender area. Encourage your partner from the beginning and remind them throughout the massage to let you know how they are feeling. It's important to have your partner communicate when something's feeling really good as well. Then you can explore more sweet spots in that general area and give it even more loving touch.

In all my years of teaching and practice, I have never seen anyone hurt from a massage when practicing with metta, communication, and easing in. Know that these tools are the foundations of helping you and your partner to feel better and better.

If at some point during the massage you do use too much pressure or you put your partner in too deep a stretch, because of all your efforts to communicate and ease in, in all likelihood they will forgive you and encourage you to continue. That is because you have created a mutually beneficial massage that is tapping into divine love and profound respect.

What Does It Mean to Ease In?

There are a three principles of easing in you should know before beginning. They come up again and again.

Principle 1—Move from Lighter to Deeper Pressure

Before you begin your massage, one of the first questions you'll ask your partner is how much pressure they like. Usually I ask on a scale of one to ten, with ten being the deepest. Then I do a little squeeze test to make sure that we are on the same page.

That is the start of the pressure conversation, but it is by no means the end. Depending on the part of the body you're massaging, and any issues that may be going on in that part of the body, the ideal pressure will vary. It's just one reason that, with any massage technique or stretch, you should start with much lighter pressure than their perceived maximum and gradually increase from there. This will give you the space to ask questions, to see how things are feeling, and make adjustments as needed.

It's similar to adding salt to a recipe. It's always preferable to add a little at a time to get to that desired taste. If you put in too much too fast, then it is much harder to reverse course. For example, say your partner likes a pretty strong massage, eight out of ten, and you have a clear understanding of what that means, then you would start much lighter, such as a three out of ten, and gradually increase the pressure with each repetition.

Principle 2—Use Repetition and Pauses

There are a couple of aspects to this principle that need exploring. The first is the idea of pausing. Pauses are another vital secret to giving an incredible massage. What it means is that once you find that ideal spot, stretch or pressure, then you should hold it for a certain length of time.

It is in those pauses that the magic takes place. The deeper truth about massage is that all those receiving benefits do not come from you, the giver. They come from the receiver and their body's ability to heal itself. Our body's ability to heal itself is nothing new. In fact, it is something it does every night when you sleep as it recovers from the activities of the day.

When you touch an area of the body, you are bringing awareness to that part of the body so that it can take over and bring its internal pharmacy of medicine to the scene. Pausing allows for that to happen. Pausing also allows your partner the opportunity to breathe more deeply, to enjoy the great sensations you're bringing their way, and to relax into what they are feeling.

Given that we have more than thirty-seven trillion cells in the body, and that they are in regular communication, our body is able to process trillions of bits of information every single second. We are the most powerful supercomputers on the planet. Therefore, those pauses do not have to be long at all for all those benefits to take effect. One or two seconds might be all the body needs.

Keeping that in mind, here's a general guideline for how to work with pausing in your massage:

1. Gradually ease in.
2. Pause one to two seconds.
3. Gradually ease out.
4. Repeat steps one through three and pause, for the same length of time, or longer; perhaps three to four seconds.
5. Repeat steps one to three again as needed and possibly extend those pauses.

The decision to lengthen those pauses varies from person to person. When you are working on someone who is stiff, has an injury, has a hard time, you'll often want to keep working with shorter pauses. When someone is able to relax into the massage, then lengthen the pauses.

More often than not, your partner will be able to relax into what you're doing, and you can lengthen those pauses. Sometimes that could mean a pause of five seconds, sometimes thirty seconds or more. The area you're massaging and the technique you're using also directly impacts how long to extend those pauses. I'll help to clarify the length of those pauses once I start describing specific parts of the massage.

The massage you are learning here has both a stretching and a passive receiving component. In both cases, whether you are massaging muscles or putting someone into a stretch, you'll want to start with a shorter pause and potentially move into longer pauses with each repetition.

I like to start with short pauses and light pressure no matter who I am massaging, whether that person is young and fit, flexible, and likes deep pressure, or is stiff and in pain. I think it's clear why you would ease in for a stiffer person, but even for someone who is flexible, there are parts of their body that may be stiff that they are not currently aware of. There may be muscles that don't get a lot of attention and this approach will help you to cover them all.

The point of this principle is to ease in by using repetition to massage or stretch the body and deepen the experience by using longer pauses as needed.

Principle 3—Walk up and down the Ladder of Pressure

One way to look at the options you have in applying pressure is as though they exist on a ladder. Lighter aspects are the first steps of the ladder and the deepest ones are at the top.

In "How slow can you go, how high can you fly," you start from the bottom of the ladder and gradually work your way up. Lighter pressure into deeper pressure and shorter pauses into longer pauses are two ways to move up the ladder.

To this list, we need to add the various massage techniques at your disposal when it is time to massage those muscles. One of the fun things about Thai Massage that also makes it easier to give is that you can use various parts of your body as a massage tool. Your hands, thumbs, forearms, elbows, knees, feet, even your head are all at your disposal. The massage you're learning in this program utilizes your palms, fists, thumbs, and feet.

Rung 1: Circles, Back and Forth Movements, Sweeping

The lightest kind of touch is close to the skin level. Light circles and gentle back and forth movements help you to get to know the area you are about to massage. They also help your partner to relax into the massage. I often think of it as melting the tension in the area. You are softening, you are exploring and, as such, it is an incredibly valuable part of the massage.

When I massage the shoulders, the back, or really any area of the body, I don't just start from these gentle movements, I return often. The massage is an interplay between going lighter and deeper and back again. The more tension spots you discover, the stiffer your partner, or the lighter they prefer their pressure, the more often you'll likely return to these gentle movements. Lighter does not mean less effective. In fact, the more space you find for these lighter movements the more powerful your massage becomes.

Sweeping means to use your hands to stroke the area with relatively gentle movements. It is a gentle yet incredibly powerful way to send feelings of relaxation to your partner. Think about it, when was the last time you were swept? It is one of the most nurturing ways to touch another person, a way that unlocks powerful waves of relaxation, especially when done in combination with your intentional rocking movements.

While the whole massage is a way of sharing metta, in many cases you can ramp up that experience when you sweep. Set your intention toward loving kindness and compassion as you sweep the area you were just massaging. The general rule of thumb regarding sweeping is there can never be enough of it. And you generally sweep at the end of every massage technique.

Rung 2: Side to Side Movements (Chasing)

Chasing means to use your side rock and apply pressure with one side of your body. For example, you lean to your right and make contact with your right palm. Then lean to the other side and apply pressure with your left palm. I call this chasing, as if your right hand is chasing your left hand or vice versa. This technique helps you to sink more deeply into the muscles, but at the same time you are limited in how deep you can press since there's only so much leverage available to you when using side rock.

Rung 3: Back and Forth Movements (Hopping)

Hopping means to use forward rock to massage an area, and when you do so you are using your whole body to help apply the pressure. As such, you have the full range of gravity, leverage, and body weight at your disposal, if needed. I call this hopping because you are like a kangaroo or a bunny rabbit applying pressure with two hands (or feet or fists) at the same time.

Within these three rungs there is the potential for limitless variation once you include the first two principles of moving from lighter to deeper pressure and going from shorter to longer pauses.

Massaging with Your Hands

When using your hands, you can use the fleshy part of your palm closest to your wrist, the back of your hand, in between the big knuckles (called soft fists) or your thumbs.

When it comes to giving massage, your hands are the most vulnerable part of your body and therefore the part that is most easily prone to injury. The ways in which to protect them are twofold. On the one hand (pun intended), know how to use them safely. On the other, don't overuse them. Interchange parts of your hands along with other parts of your body as massage tools as needed so as not to tire out any individual part. What makes giving the massage feel good—while keeping it interesting—is getting comfortable using all the parts of your body available to you.

To start this practice, place a pillow or a folded blanket in front of you. If you're on the ground sit in kneeling diamond. If you're going to practice on a bed, then put the pillow on the bed and stand comfortably.

Palms

How to safely use the palm of your hand.

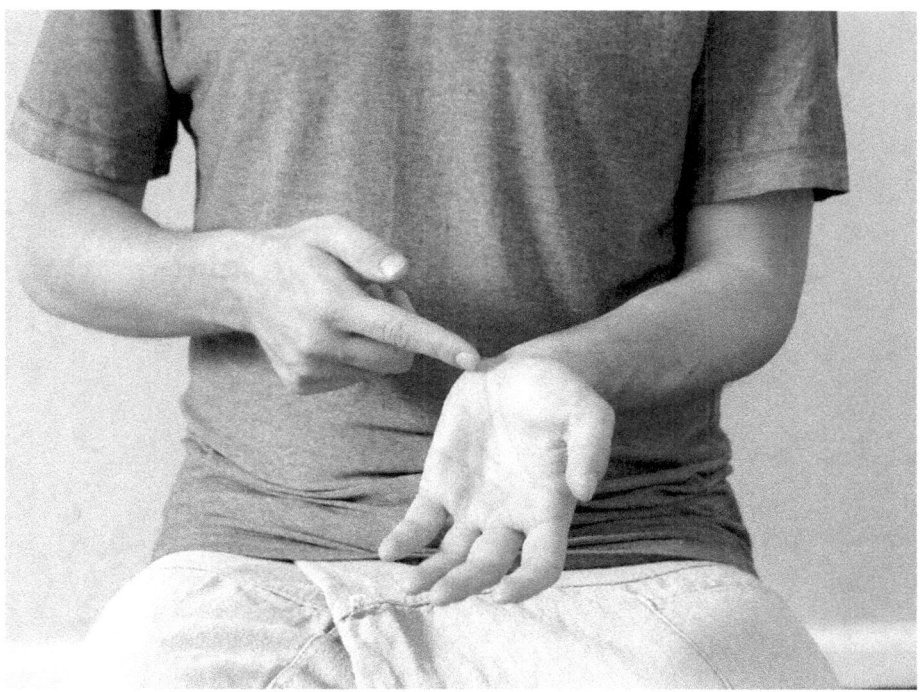

When using your palm, use the part with the most padding, which is close to your wrist. Take a moment to feel your palm and locate that padded part.

From here do a little test. Put your palm face down and hold your forearm out in front of you so it is parallel to the ground. Keeping your forearm parallel to the ground, bend your wrist until you feel the first point of resistance. That does not mean bending it as far as you can, just to that first point of tension. If you're like me, then that means you can bend your wrist to about fifty to sixty degrees (Figure 1).

I have yet to meet anyone who can bend their wrist all the way to ninety degrees (Figure 2) without forcing it.

Figure 1: Wrist bent fifty degrees

Figure 2: Wrist bent ninety degrees

Therefore, if you constantly massage with your wrists bent close to ninety degrees, then you are likely to put a fair amount of pressure into your wrists and eventually they will tire of this movement.

You want to be aware of how far forward your shoulders come over your hands when you massage. You can test this by putting your hands on the far end of the pillow and rocking up and pressing into the pillow. The more forward your shoulders, the more you are bending your wrists. If you want to protect your wrists, simply don't rock as far forward and don't rely solely on your palms when you want to massage with your hands.

The different options available to you when using your palms are:

Palm Chasing Palm

Rock to one side. Apply palm pressure with the equivalent hand. Rock to the other side and repeat.

Palm Hopping

Forward rock. Apply palm pressure with both hands simultaneously. Protect your wrists: Check the angle of your wrist and avoid angles beyond eighty degrees.

Palm over Palm

Place one palm over the other to apply pressure. Your bottom hand is like a massage tool that feels for the ideal spot to apply pressure. Once found, keep it relaxed. Your top hand is your power hand. Pressure moves from the center of the body, down the arms, and through the top hand. It is an important palm- and wrist-saving technique. You will practice it when massaging the back.

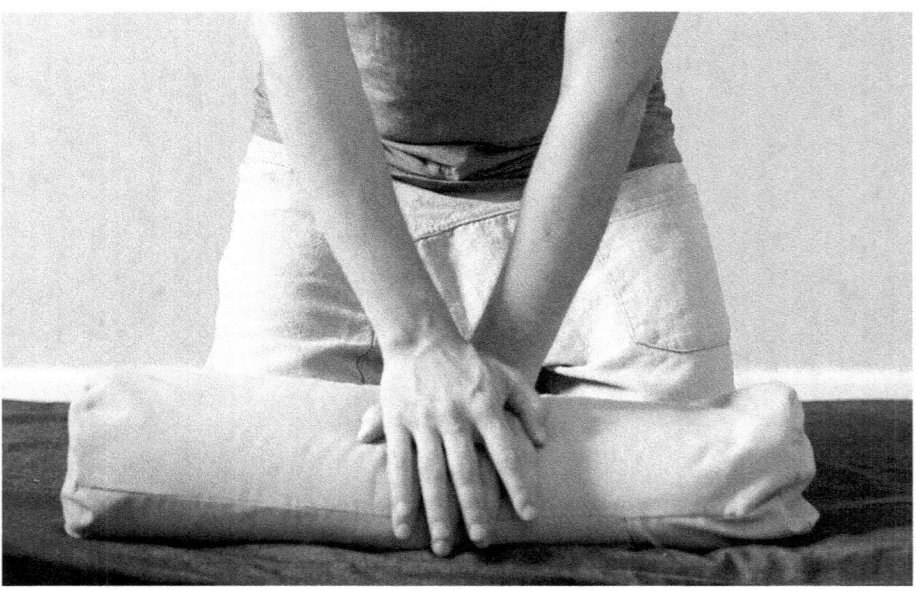

Soft Fists

Soft fists are a wonderful alternative to using your palms. You want to get comfortable massaging with your fists so that you can alternate freely between your palms and fists. This will go a huge way toward protecting your hands and wrists.

To use soft fists, make a fist. That flat area between your knuckles in the middle and the base of your fingers is the area you'll use to massage. The idea is to keep your fingers relaxed as you make the fist. Let the energy flow to the tips of your fingers. This is why it's called soft fists.

When you use soft fists, your forearms and wrists will be in a straight line. This means you'll be using entirely different muscles in your hands, wrists and forearms than you would with palming. Usually your fists will also be turned out, similar to their position on a steering wheel when driving a car.

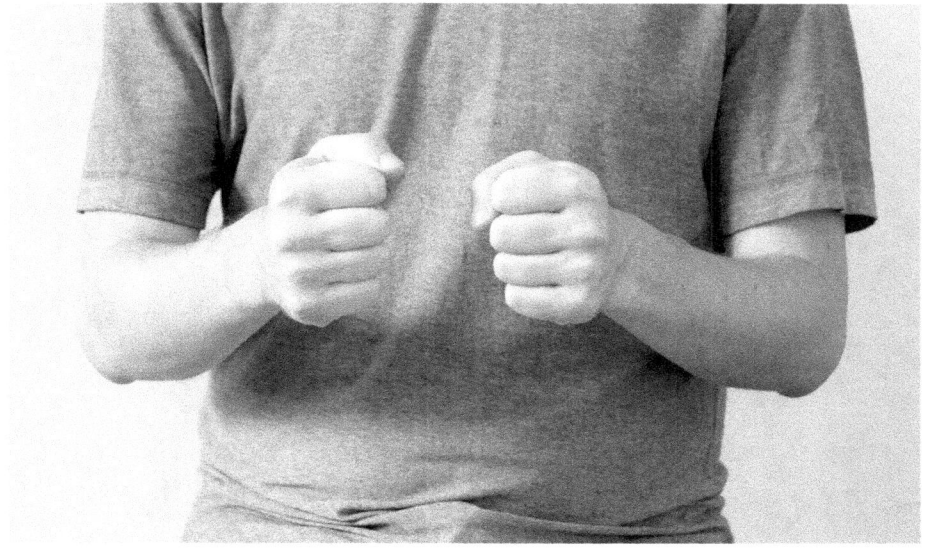

Fist Chasing Fist

Keep your fists and fingers relaxed. Rock to one side. Apply pressure with the equivalent fist. Rock to the other side and repeat.

Fist Hopping

Keep your fists and fingers relaxed. Forward rock and let your fist make contact with the massage area. Your fists are in a straight line with your wrists.

Thumbs

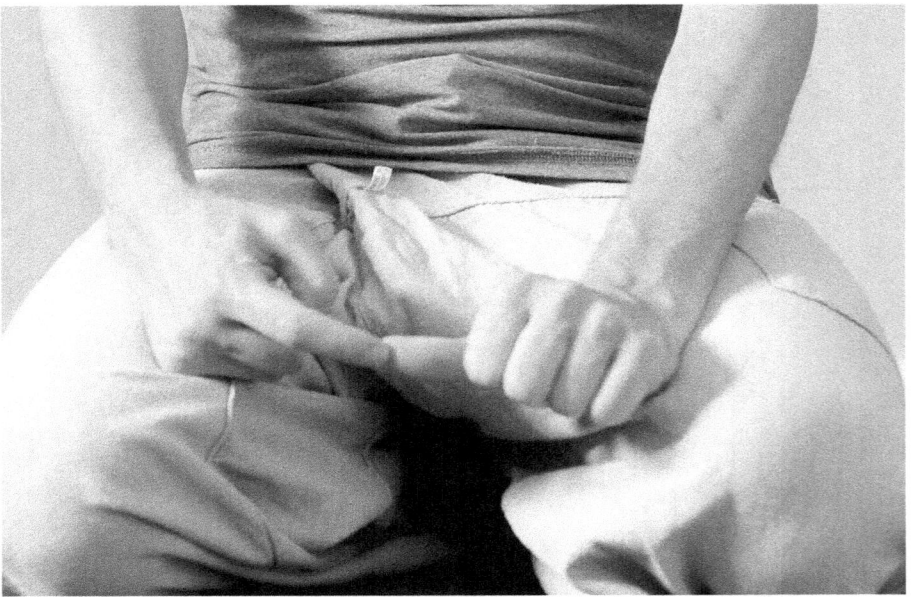

Your thumbs are the most vulnerable part of your body when it comes to massaging, specifically the joint at the base that joins your thumb to the rest of your hand. That is why in general I discourage using your thumbs independently of each other when giving the massage, especially in combination with forward rock, which uses more of your body weight. In this program, we will use the thumbs to help massage the back, and we will use a technique called palm over thumb to help you use your thumbs wisely.

When you do use your thumbs, the part to use is the most padded part, about halfway between the tip of your thumb and center line. Take a moment to locate and feel the most padded part of your thumb. When using your thumb, keep it relaxed and relatively close to the rest of your hand, at about a thirty-to-forty-degree angle. The farther your thumb is from your hand, the greater the potential to put a lot of pressure on the base.

Palm over Thumb

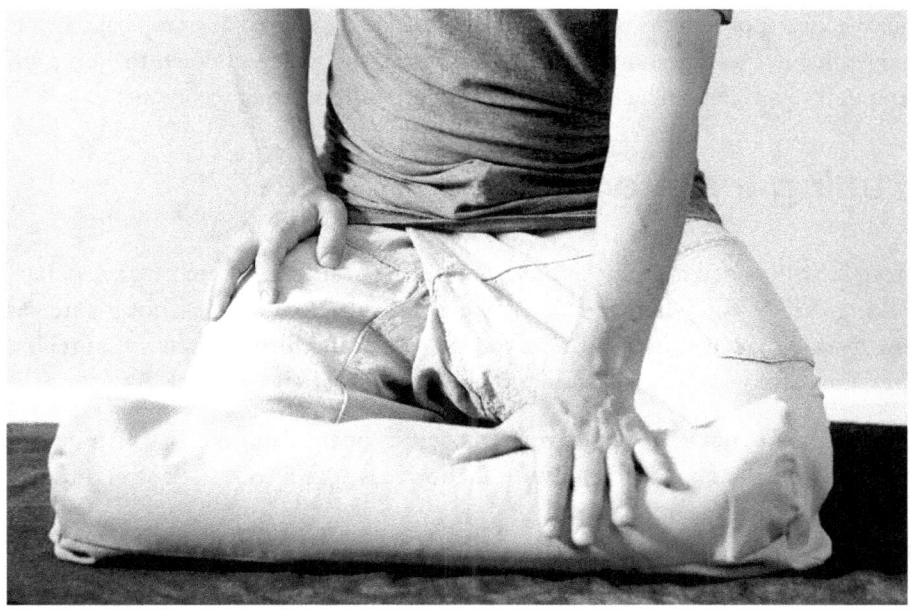

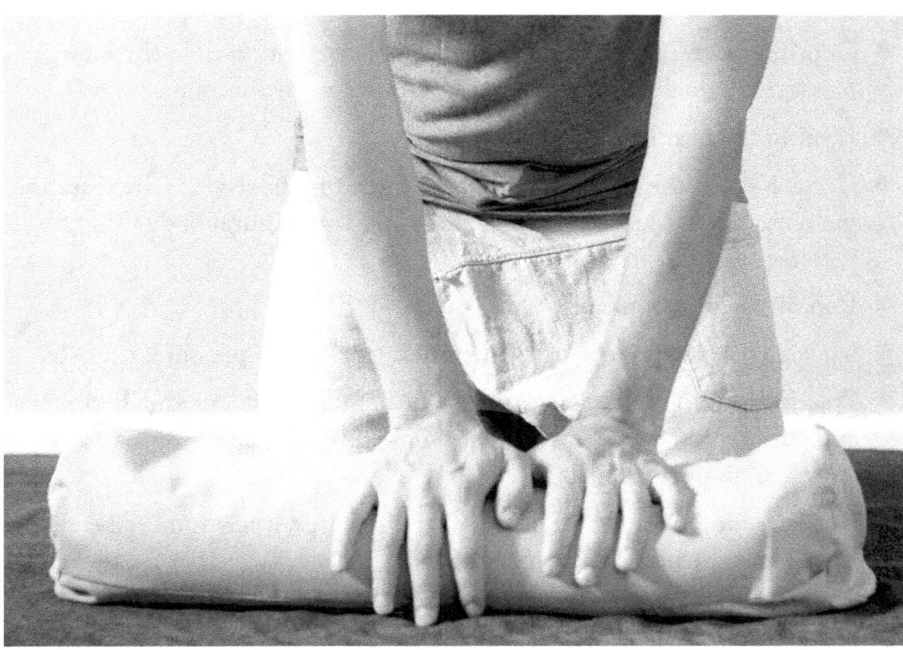

Place your thumb so that it sticks out from the hand at about a thirty-degree angle. Place your palm over your thumb. Your bottom hand is like a massage tool that feels for the ideal spot to apply pressure. Once found, keep it relaxed. Your top hand is your power hand. Pressure moves from the center of the body and down the arms and comes through the top hand. It is an important thumb-saving technique.

Putting It All Together

Your first massage is going to be to the pillow or blanket which works so hard taking care of you when you sleep. The pillow never complains, but it sure can use a good massage! Imagine that your pillow would like an eight out of ten for pressure, and you did a pressure test so you know what that feels like.

If you're on a mat or bed, position yourself in open diamond. If you're next to the bed, then stand comfortably and in both cases, feel your back straight, neck long, and shoulders relaxed.

- Place your hands over the far edge of the pillow.
- Start with gentle circles or back and forth motions (a one out of ten for pressure).
- Continue with palm chasing palm: Lean to one side with a three for pressure, gradually sink in and pause for one to two seconds.
- Lean to the next side and repeat.
- Come back to the first side and pause three to four seconds. Increase the pressure to a five just by pausing and using your natural body weight to increase the pressure.
- Repeat on the second side.
- Make gentle circles to prepare the pillow for deeper pressure.
- Practice palm hopping: Rock up to kneeling diamond, gradually sink in and pause for one to two seconds, which increases the pressure to a six and then gradually ease out.
- Repeat palm hopping and pause for five seconds, using your body weight to increase the pressure to an eight.
- Complete the massage by sweeping.
- Repeat the same sequence using fist chasing fist and fist hopping.

This exercise is designed to show you the ways to walk up the ladder to gradually increase the pressure and deepen the massage. But keep in mind that there are many variations within this framework. You will learn how to vary your approach depending on the needs of your partner.

Now that you've practiced on a pillow, you're just about ready to practice on your partner. Just one more step to go, and it's another great secret to giving an incredible massage.

CHAPTER 14

COMMUNICATING SAFETY & COMFORT FOR AN OPTIMAL MASSAGE

There is more to giving an incredible massage than the massage itself. That's just as true massaging your loved ones as it would be giving a massage in exchange for money. Since you're touching some of the most important people in your life, the argument can be made that this component is even more vital when those are the people you'll be massaging. This section gives tips on how to create a safe and nurturing environment in which to give your massage.

In the last chapter we talked about communication being one of the great secrets to giving an incredible massage. This chapter expands upon all the ways to practice communication with your partner. Perhaps the first thing to consider if you're massaging friends and family members—beyond someone you're learning this course with—is how to describe the massage. In order for someone to agree to the experience, think of how you can speak their language to get them excited.

When going through this exercise, think of someone in your life that you'd like to massage and how you will talk to them. For example, if you want to massage your aunt Esther and you know that she has a lot of shoulder and back tension, then my suggestion is to describe the massage as something that can do wonders for her back and shoulders. If you are massaging your sister Candace and you know she loves having her feet massaged, then let her know there is a great foot massage component.

Once your partner has agreed to the massage, it could be a good idea to send them an email reminder, a personal note that touches on the time, the place, and how they can prepare for the massage.

In this massage, your partner keeps their clothes on, so they will need to wear comfortable clothing that will allow for them to be stretched. It is best to receive this massage on a fairly empty stomach, so ideally your partner shouldn't eat or drink for at least thirty minutes before the session. You could also include a short description of what to expect in the massage, similar to how you described it to them originally so that it speaks to their needs and wants. It is also a great idea to ask if there's anything you should know about their body ahead of time.

During the massage, there are many conscious and subtle ways to support your partner and to communicate that support and love.

Some of the Things to Consider Include:

- The tools you bring into your massage space
- The massage environment
- Questions to ask before the massage begins
- Questions to ask during the massage
- What to do once the massage ends

If you want to provide an outstanding experience that is nurturing, relaxing, meditative, and loving, you should consider that your massage starts as soon as you set a time and date and it ends a couple of days after the conclusion of the session. The more you think about all the facets of giving and how to personalize it, the better it's likely to be.

Setting up Your Massage Space

I am a big believer in comfort. The more things you have on hand to help make your partner comfortable, the better. At the top of that list has to be something great to lie on. If you're going to be giving the massage on a bed, then you should be all set. Make sure to have a chair nearby for you to sit on as well.

If you're going to give the massage on a mat on the ground, then there are many options out there. The most basic would be a plush carpet. Another would be a couple of yoga mats touching side-by-side with four to five blankets on top.

If you want to give massages on the ground regularly, then it is worth investing in a good massage mat. Having something that is comfortable for you, that is supportive to your knees and body, and comfortable for your partner is going to make the experience that much more inviting for everyone involved. There are many massage mats out there. Those include foam mats, futons, gym mats, Thai mats from Thailand that are filled with kapok (cotton batting), and memory foam. Costs typically range from $100-$400 or more.

I make my own mat, which is called the Metta Massage Mat. I designed it with your knees and body in mind. It is portable, weighing eight pounds, and the foam core cushions your knees (and by extension, your back) while you massage. The mat also comes with a lifetime guarantee not to wear out. I love the mat, and I think it is the best option on which to practice comfortably on the ground. But a mat is an investment, so pick the one that speaks to you and your body. If you're going to be massaging one primary person, then it's a good idea to involve them in the decision as well. It is always a great idea to check out a few different options before making your final choice.

Other Things to Include in Your Massage Space:

- Pillows of varying size and firmness
- Two rolled up towels or buckwheat bolsters
- Two or more blankets
- Tissues

The more of these items you have the better. The point of these props is to help both you and your partner be as comfortable as possible. Placing rolled-up towels or bolsters under the feet or head when lying face down can go a long way toward making a luxurious experience.

Pillows under the tummy, knees, or legs can support people with sensitive backs or bonier hips. Using pillows to help create some comforting distance between the two of you can also be very important to let everyone breathe more easily. Using these props will be discussed in greater detail in the next chapter as we describe the massage techniques.

I like to cover the part of my partner I am not massaging with a blanket. Body temperature typically drops when receiving a massage, so this will prevent them from getting cold. If your partner is cold when receiving, it makes relaxing into the massage more of a challenge, and once they feel cold it can take a fair amount of time for them to warm back up.

Tissues are there in case there is an emotional release. If that were to happen during your massage, usually it is a good idea to stop the treatment and give your partner a moment to gather themselves and decide if they want to continue.

The Massage Environment

This massage can be given just about anywhere. On a bed, in a multi-purpose room with the TV going, or in a serene, calm, and meditative space.

My preference and recommendation would be to create a dedicated massage space. A place where you retreat from the outer world and into your space of relaxation. I know that is not always possible. In those instances, taking a few moments to convert your shared space into a tranquil room will certainly be worth the effort.

I have heard of many stories from students who put a lot of thought and wonderful touches into making that personal and peaceful space. Some of those details include:

- The color scheme of the room
- Statues, pictures, artwork on the walls
- Flowers and plants
- Candles
- A clean and tidy area
- Soothing scents, perhaps with the help of a diffuser
- Water flowing, such as with a plug in mini-waterfall
- Music that fits the moment

These touches should be a creative endeavor. Bring your own heart and style into it.

Have a variety of music options to choose from. Music really does help set the mood. It is great to have music that you'll enjoy massaging along with. Have playlists or radio stations with music that you like. And within that variety, ask for your partner's input on what they'd like to listen to. If they say they don't care, you might still want to ask if they prefer something instrumental or with lyrics. Sometimes lyrics can be distracting.

If you want to help your partner slow down, then calmer music will usually help. If you want to bring more energy to the massage, then have more uplifting music. Having appropriate music can be of great service toward accomplishing your massage goals. It makes the exchange fun and augments the flowing quality of the massage.

Questions to Ask Before the Massage Starts

Your massage starts the moment you schedule it. If you're making a future plan to massage someone, then ask your partner if there's anything you should know about ahead of time. If they mention an ailment you're not familiar with, always give yourself permission to decline the massage. Be straightforward and let them know why you are declining. If it's because you don't want to accidentally hurt or worsen the ailment, then it is good to let them know.

If they tell you something you're not familiar with, asking in advance gives you time to do research and educate yourself in what to do. Use the internet, ask people in your social network, and get in touch with us. You can post your questions on our blog or on our Facebook page, and we'll be there to help.

You may also want to have your partner get the permission of a doctor before consenting to the massage. If you're in doubt if your partner should be receiving a massage, then err on the side of caution and ask them to seek out that permission.

Before you start asking questions, take time to observe their mood, their dress, their mannerisms, and their speech to get a read on how your partner is doing and the words you'll need to help them relax and get ready.

If you sense that your partner is nervous about the massage, explain what the massage is about to help them relax. Coach them on how you intend to communicate. Let them know that you intend to check in regularly to see how they're feeling, and that you like to work with light pressure first and will gradually increase it to their liking so that everything feels good. Let them know that you encourage their feedback, both when something feels great and if they're uncomfortable with anything, and you'll make adjustments as necessary.

There are at least three questions that you should ask and expand on before beginning the massage.

How Are You?

This is an obvious question, but an important one to subconsciously let your partner know that you are paying attention, and it is also one that helps put people at ease.

Physically, Is There Anything I Should Know?

One thing to consider with this question is that many people will hold back some important information. Therefore, it is important to have a few follow up questions to get more information. A few good follow-up questions would be:

- Any recent injuries?
- Any older injuries?
- Any new activities or exercises?
- If they do mention an injury or an area they want you to focus on, then take the time to gently feel the area so you know exactly where the issue is.

From here ask them to demonstrate their mobility. For example, for neck issues ask them to look right and left and make half circles. For lower back issues, perhaps ask them to twist, turn, and lean forward and back.

Give a brief overview of the parts of the body you will work on with the reminder that if there are any areas they'd like you to skip they can tell you now or during the massage. For example, face and hair are areas that some people may not want you to touch. This is a way to bring it up without drawing attention to any particular area.

On a Scale of One to Ten, What Kind of Pressure Do You Like?

Discuss pressure on a scale of one to ten, and then do a brief pressure test to gauge that your definition of light-medium-deep matches theirs. It could be squeezing their forearm, foot, shoulders, or other part.

If your partner says they like an eight out of ten, and your ability to squeeze the forearm registers as something less than their desired pressure, then don't force it. This test is just meant to get you on the same page. When you give the massage, you'll be using more of your body weight and different techniques and parts of your body, so you'll be able to adjust accordingly.

Get to Know Their Relationship to Pain

At the same time that you are asking these questions and observing your partner, on a more subconscious level get a sense of their relationship to pain. Pain in and of itself is neither a positive or negative thing. It is simply our body's physical response to certain experiences.

A massage involving deep pressure and stretching is often about exploring their edge. If that is the approach you are taking, then your partner needs to have a positive relationship to "delicious pain." They need to feel that a little gradual pain is a good thing, and most importantly they can breathe easily even if it hurts a little.

But not all massages need to be experienced this way to be effective. At heart, this is an energetic massage and needs to be experienced as something positive for the body to release all of its natural ability to help itself. A lighter massage can be even more effective than a deep massage when this is your approach. If your partner is very sensitive to pain and discomfort, or if they seem nervous, then keep things very light and easy and make sure there is lots of communication. Let them know that you'll be checking in regularly and invite their feedback as well.

How to Ask about Pressure

When you check in during the massage, be mindful that when you ask an open-ended question, you should expect an open-ended answer. If you ask, "How's the pressure?" the common response is, "It's good." That does not tell you very much. If you catch yourself asking an open-ended question, then have a follow-up such as, "Would you like more pressure?" If you can get your partner to answer with *yes* or *no* responses, or with their specific likes and dislikes, it will give you better guidance on how to adjust.

Remember to Check in Regularly

Some times to check-in are at the start with your first few touches, when turning your partner over, when massaging and stretching areas that push limits, and especially when massaging tension or problem areas that require greater attention.

What to Do Once the Massage Ends

Once the massage ends, it is a good idea to have a drink waiting nearby, either water or calming tea that is not too hot.

Let your partner know that it is a good idea to drink more than their regular amount of water for the next twenty-four hours to help their body flush toxins. You can encourage and participate in relaxing activities together, such as taking a walk, enjoying a healthy meal, or taking a bath.

> **The benefits and after effects of a massage can sometimes be felt for several days following a session.**

Not all of the effects are ones of ease and relaxation. Sometimes people report feeling groggy, tired, sore, headachy, and so on. These are all regular side effects from receiving, usually a result of the body detoxifying and healing itself. It is a good idea to let your partner know that if they experience any of these side effects after the massage that it is normal.

And it's greatly important to check in on your partner the next day. This little extra step goes a long way toward showing support and care for your loved one.

CHAPTER 15

Massage Facing Up

This massage is divided into two parts; face up and face down. They are interchangeable. If your partner prefers to start facing down, then start with the next chapter.

Each technique includes a description of setting up on a mat. At the end of the section is a description for any modifications when massaging on a bed or massage table.

Each technique also includes important pointers regarding the benefits, considerations for their comfort and safety, ideas for how to ease in (or how slow can you go), and consideration for your own safety and comfort.

It covers many different situations, and every effort is made to be as thorough as possible to help you teach yourself how to give each technique. If there are some aspects that are unique to you and your needs that are not explained here, then feel free to reach out to us by emailing **info@stillightcentre.com**.

Download your own PDF workbook here **shaiplonski.sendlane.com/view/compassionate-touch-landing-page** so you can take notes and have a handy reference guide that you can print out and have next to you as you practice the massage.

Beginning the Massage

Begin your massage by inviting your partner to lie down on their back and take a moment to help them feel comfortable. When lying face up, that may include a pillow under the head and pillows under one or both legs. As a general rule, I like to cover the part of the body I'm not massaging, either with a sheet or a blanket.

Take a moment to bring that first pillar of meditation and metta into the massage. Sit quietly, perhaps with hands together in front of your heart in a prayer pose. Take some nice breaths and send some feelings of love and compassion toward your partner. It can also be a great idea to set an intention for your massage. That could be something general, such as to help them relax or something more specific such as helping to bring relief to a particular part of the body that is experiencing stress.

As you give your massage, keep coming back to your intention as a guide and as a way to deepen the metta experience.

Leg Shake

A great way to relax the back, legs, and body.

Transition: Sit in diamond stance with their heels resting on your lap in the palms of your hand.

Posture:

- Keeping your hands and their legs on your lap, move your body from side to side.
- Bend your elbows, raise their legs, and keep your arms by your side to shake the legs with a multitude of variations: juggle the legs, twist feet back and forth, and encourage the whole back to move.
- Lean back to traction the legs for five to ten seconds. Repeat two to three times.

Benefits:

- Relaxes the back, legs, head, and body.
- Circulates blood and oxygen.
- Helps to raise energy.

How slow can you go:

- Starting with their legs on your lap and shaking your body from side to side is a gentle way to begin for both you and your partner.
- Once you lift the legs, begin with slow shakes and small circles.
- Increase the speed and size of circles for more flexible partners.

For their safety and comfort:

Your aim is to provide movement in the body from the feet up to the head. But if your partner is stiff, keep it slow and gentle and check in to make sure it is comfortable for their back. Stiffer clients usually get a lot of benefits from pulling back for the leg traction. You may want to repeat the traction five or more times, working with shorter pauses of two to three seconds, before extending into the five to ten second range.

For your safety and comfort:

Legs can be heavy! Shaking the legs with your lap may be the only variation to choose if you find their legs too heavy to lift.

Similarly, doing this for too long can require plenty of work for your body as you hold the legs with bent elbows. Keep your arms close to your body and only shake for a few seconds. To extend the time you give this posture, put the legs back on your lap and shake a second time. Repeat the transition between legs on lap and then by your side as many times as necessary.

If the legs are too heavy for you to place on your lap, then it is better to skip this posture.

On a bed or massage table:

Your position will depend on the size relationship between you and your partner and the bed. You could sit on a chair or stand behind the bed or table. You could also get on the bed and position yourself in diamond stance.

Knee to Chest

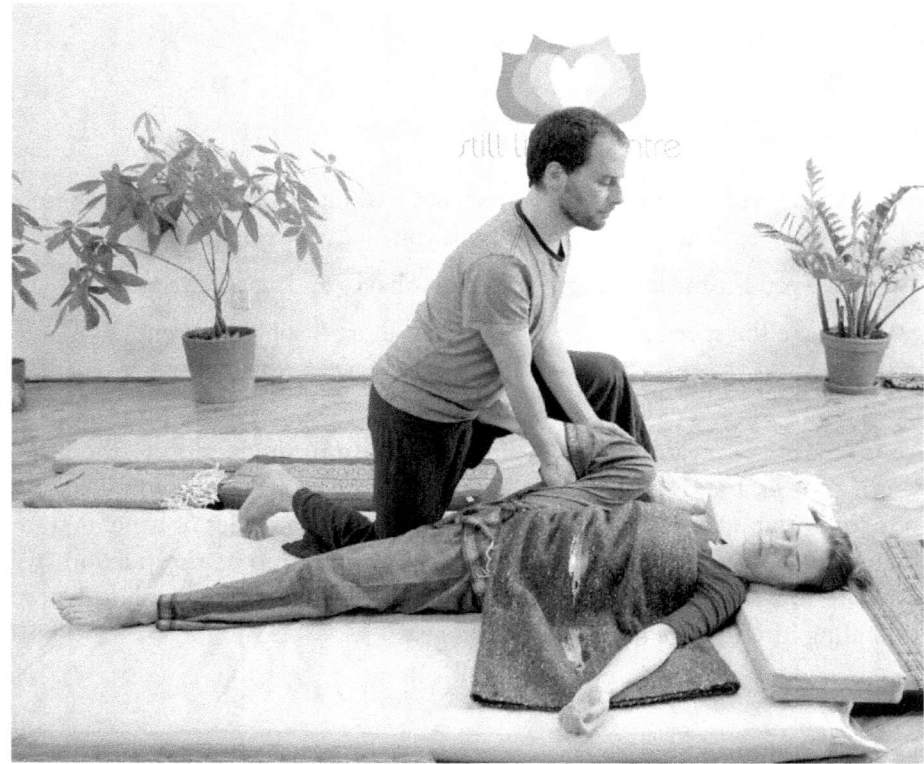

An all-in-one stretch for the hip, lower back, and hamstrings.

Transition:

- Holding one leg, put one hand under their heel and one under or close to the knee.
- Elevate from diamond to warrior and bend their knee to a ninety-degree angle.
- Place their foot in the hip crease of your warrior leg (your outside leg).
- Glide your warrior forward close enough so that the foot and leg would remain in place if you were to let go with your hands.

Posture:

First version: body only

- Use forward rock so that your body pushes their leg forward into the stretch.
- Release the stretch by rocking back and repeat.
- Start with one to three second pauses and increase for five or up to ten seconds as they relax into it.

Second version: body and soft fists

- Continue by simultaneously rocking forward and using soft fists (one or two hands at a time depending on what you can comfortably reach) to press on the back of the thigh.
- Start by pressing close to the knee. Release the stretch by rocking back and repeat, moving your hands one or two spots up and down the back of the leg.
- Repeat by finding a different angle and helping to direct the leg further in or away from the midline.

Benefits:

- Stretches the hip flexors, lower back, hamstrings.
- Stimulates digestion and massages internal organs.

How slow can you go:

- Ease in by having short pauses of about one to two seconds before long holds of five seconds or more.
- Only increase the pauses for more flexible partners. You may want to check in as you decide to increase the length of pause.
- The first version without the use of your fists to press on the back of the legs is lighter, so start there and then move on to the second variation.

For their safety and comfort:

Allow them to control the direction their leg wants to go. The name, knee to chest, is misleading. The knee does not have to touch the chest, and often the leg wants to be directed to the outside of the body. Get feedback to make sure each direction you choose to take the leg is comfortable. That is especially true with the leg close to the midline, as this can pinch the hip flexors.

For your safety and comfort:

Generally, you need to glide your warrior pretty far forward to use your body to help engage the stretch. Use one or two soft fists to press on their leg, whichever is more comfortable.

On a bed or massage table:

- This can be done on a bed if you feel comfortable to be in a warrior stance on a mattress.
- This can also be done with you standing next to the bed or massage table as long as your partner is close to the edge.
  - Stand next to the bed or massage table in Tai Chi pose with one of your legs in front and the other behind.
  - Raise their leg with one hand on top of their knee and the other on the heel for the lighter version.
  - Keep one hand on the knee and use soft fists on the back of the thigh for the deeper version.

Straight Leg Stretch

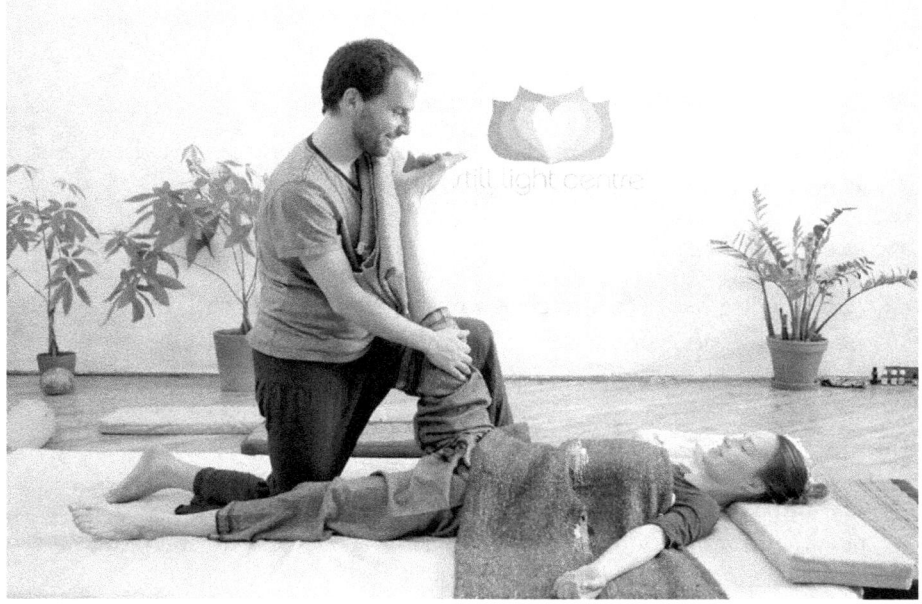

Another all-in-one stretch that targets the hamstrings, calf, and foot muscles.

Transition:

- Move back a little.
- Sit down in diamond.
- Place their leg on your outside shoulder.
- Place one hand on their thigh just above the knee and the other on the bottom of the foot.
- For less flexible clients, stay seated in a diamond stance.
- For more flexible clients, raise up to warrior and advance up to a maximum where their leg is at a ninety-degree angle with their body.

Posture:

First version: leg only

- Rock forward to stretch the leg.
- Start with a two or three second pause.
- Release and repeat the stretch three more times, lengthening the pauses as needed up to ten seconds or more.

Second version: leg and foot

- After the leg has been stretched a few times, hold the stretch for several seconds and press down on the ball of the foot.
- Release and repeat the foot stretch.

Third version: deeper leg stretch

- If your partner wants a deeper stretch beyond the ninety-degree angle, take the foot off your shoulder and push the heel and leg forward as far as it's comfortable for both of you.

Benefits: Stretches the hamstrings, calf, foot, and lower back.

How slow can you go:

- Start with a depth that is not their deepest stretch and hold it for one to two seconds.
- Release and repeat.
- Start to adjust the depth of the stretch and the length of the hold. You can work your way into holding the stretch for ten to twenty seconds for more flexible partners or keep it in the one to two second range for tighter legs and hamstrings.

For their safety and comfort:

For many people, the sitting in diamond version which raises their leg to about forty-five degrees may be deep enough. This can be a very deep stretch for the leg and back, so check in as you explore their edge of flexibility, especially if your partner is stiff or has a history of injuries or stiffness in this area of the body.

For your safety and comfort:

Depending on your size relationship, you may decide to rest their foot on your shoulder, on your upper chest, or in your hands. It is best when your body can support the leg rather than your hands. If it ends up that the foot is on your chest and you would rather not have direct contact in that manner, then place a blanket over your shoulder to create separation between their leg and your body.

On a bed or massage table:

- This posture can be done on a bed as long as you are comfortable in warrior.
- Version one and three can also be done with you standing next to the bed or massage table as long as your partner is close to the edge.
  - Stand next to the bed in Tai Chi stance with one of your legs in front and the other behind.
  - Raise their leg with one hand on top of their thigh just above the knee and the other on the back of the heel.
  - Ease them into and out of the stretch starting with one or two second pauses and making adjustments from there.

CHAPTER 16

MASSAGING FACING DOWN

Take a moment to help the person you're massaging feel comfortable. When lying face down that may include bolsters or rolled-up towels placed in an upside-down V to support the neck and head or pillows under the abdomen, waist, and feet.

Sole Walk

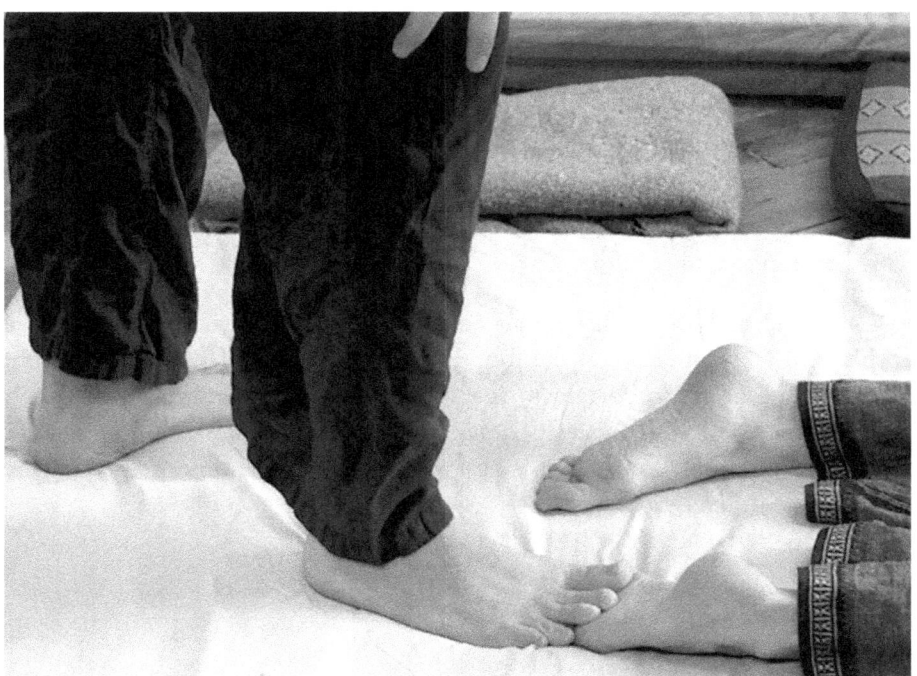

Use your feet to give a great foot massage.

Transition:

- If you started face-up, then ask your partner to turn over and place bolsters or rolled-up towels in a reverse V shape to support the head, neck, and shoulders lying face down (see back massage for a picture of the bolster placement).
- Place a pillow under the abdomen and/or hips for added comfort as needed.
- Adjust their feet so that the big toes point toward each other and there is about a fist- or foot-width of distance between them.

Posture:

- Walk on the feet one at a time.
- Face forward using the ball of your foot.
- You can walk over the feet including the toes, ball of the foot, and the main part of the foot—just don't step on their heel.
- Develop your sensitivity and range of pressure. With each new place on the foot, begin with a feather-light touch.
- Release and repeat in the same spot and slowly sink in and increase the pause.
- Repeat by finding new places to walk on the foot.

Benefits: Massages the foot, relaxes the legs and back, and affects all of the reflexology points on the body.

For their safety and comfort:

For stiff feet and ankles, keep a rolled-up hand towel in your massage space to place in the gap between the foot and mat. With all of your body weight at your disposal, it's important to start with very light pressure to allow their foot muscles to relax. If they experience a foot cramp, then pause the massage. Usually if the foot cramps up, it is best to move on to the other foot or to the next part of the massage.

For your safety and comfort:

For greater control and the potential to increase pressure if needed, keep a hand on your thigh as you press in.

How slow can you go:

- There are so many wonderful spots you can find when working with your feet. The goal is to develop the same sensitivity in using your feet as you would with your hands.
- Start with a light touch and, as gradually as you can, sink into the soft tissue inch by inch.
- When you find a good spot, start with a short pause of one to two seconds, release and repeat and possibly start to increase the pause to five seconds or more.

On a bed or massage table:

Sit on the bed or on a chair, and use your elbow in place of the walking. Begin by giving the foot a good squeeze, and then sink in gently with your elbow. It's best not to use the tip of the elbow, rather a softer area just beyond the tip. Start with light pressure, and increase gradually with each repetition.

Back Massage

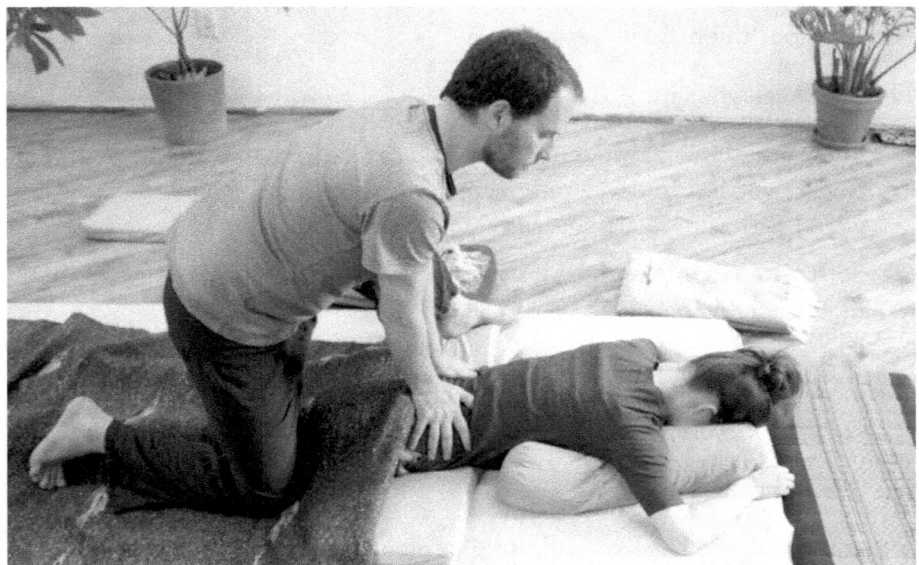

Palming the two sides of the back.

Palm over palm.

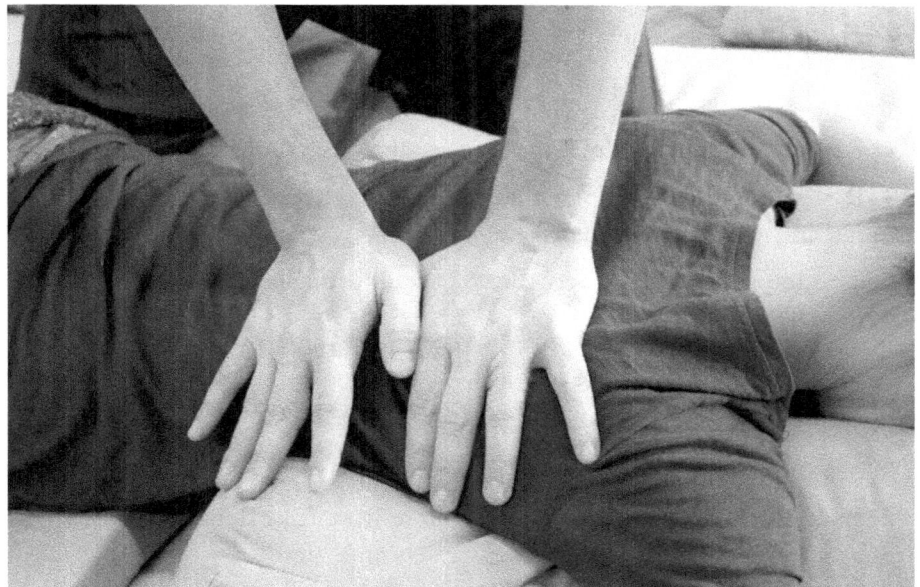

Palm over thumb.

The part of the massage many have been waiting for! Use a combination of palms, fists, and thumbs to massage the back.

Transition:

- Position yourself in a warrior stance over the low back facing your partner's head.
- Straddle the back with one knee down on one side and one foot up on the other.
- Locate the muscles that run parallel to the spine. They are about an inch away from the spine and run from the neck all the way to the low back.
- Locate the sacrum, which is a flat triangular bone all the way at the lowest part of the back.

Posture:

Version 1: both sides of the back together

- Place your hands over the sacrum and gently rock it from side to side for a few seconds.

- Place your fists or palms—slightly turned out—on either side of the sacrum.
- Make gentle circles with one hand and then the other.
- Use fist chasing fist to ease into one side of the back at a time.
- Repeat with fist or palm hopping onto the same spot.
- Repeat the three steps of circles, chasing, and hopping in different spots moving up and down the back.
- Continue until you are between the shoulder blades and then return back to the sacrum.

Version 2: one side of the back at a time, working the muscles on the far side of the spine

- Move to one side of the body.
- Position yourself in kneeling diamond or in warrior stepping over the body, in line with the low back.
- Massage the lowest part of the back—the line between sacrum and hip—using "kneading the dough" technique:
  - Place palm over palm.
  - Rock the sacrum back and forth.
  - Wrap fingers around the hip and pull the hip toward you.
  - Release and use your palm to push the muscles away from the sacrum.
- Release and repeat rocking the sacrum and kneading the dough (pulling and pushing the low back toward you and away from you) several times.
- Massage the rest of the back using a combination of palm over palm, soft fists, and palm over thumb. For the rest of the back the motion is only one direction: push the muscles away from the spine.
- Begin by softening the area, making circles or gentle back and forth movements with each spot on the back.
- Choose your technique and push the muscles down and away from the spine.
- Spend extra time around the shoulder blades and any other spots of tension, making circles and intuitively sinking into areas of greater need.

Version 3: neck and shoulder massage

- Finish with a shoulder and neck massage.
- Bring their arms by their side and return to warrior so you're centered over the body.
- Massage the shoulders and neck with your fingers and thumbs:
  - If you are massaging with your thumbs, keep your fingers relaxed and vice versa.
- Sweep the back and back body for at least twenty seconds.

Benefits:

- Sweet relief for the back and shoulders.
- Massages the internal organs.
- Expands the breath and ribcage.

How slow can you go:

Giving a great back massage is all about taking your time, listening with full body awareness, and repeat, repeat, repeat. Once you find an area that needs greater attention, the general steps include:

- Begin with gentle circles in order to ease in the pressure.
- As you massage into the muscles, increase the pressure and pause ever so slowly, paying attention to their body's signals that they can relax while the pressure deepens. If you sense muscles tightening, breath changing, or if you roll off the muscles you will be ready to respond immediately by easing up on the pressure.
- When working both sides of the back at the same time, alternate pressing on each side before you press down with both hands at the same time
- When working one side at a time take time to explore areas of tension around the shoulder blades, the middle back, and lower back. Typically, if you find one good spot, there are several more right nearby.
- Take the time to circle in with very light pressure with every new spot on the body. Start soft and easy.

When massaging the neck and the tops of the shoulders, it's important to bring the arms alongside the body so those muscles are at rest and sink in slowly with your fingertips and thumbs, taking care not to squeeze too tightly on those sensitive muscles.

For their safety and comfort:

Place a pillow under the abdomen for added lower back comfort. With so many sore, tense spots, and overworked or tired muscles, it is especially important to practice how slow can you go for the entire back massage. The mid-back around the kidneys and lower ribs can be a very tender area for many and they wouldn't necessarily notice it as compared to lower back and shoulder issues.

For your safety and comfort:

Small adjustments to your stance and alternating between kneeling diamond and warrior are essential so that you are always comfortable and facing your work. It is always worth stopping what you are doing to make these subtle adjustments. When you can massage in greater comfort, then that is exactly what comes through your hands, your body, and all your energy.

Massaging with a palm over palm or palm over thumb means that your bottom hand (either your palm or thumb) acts as a massage tool feeling the precise spot that needs attention. Once you've found it, keep that hand relaxed. Your top hand (your palm) acts as the power hand applying pressure. Similarly, it is important to stay elevated with your shoulders over your arms so that your body helps out your arms.

To save your thumbs, it is best to use them only around the shoulder blades. Stick to using fists or palms for the middle and the lower back

On a bed or massage table:

- This can be done on a bed if you are comfortable in warrior or kneeling diamond.
- Massaging one side of the back at a time can also be done standing next to the bed or massage table.

Child's Pose

A relaxing stretch for the hips, lower back, and shoulders.

Transition:

- Ask your partner to come onto their knees with knees apart.
- Ask them to go into a forward fold and place a pillow between their body and the mat if necessary.
- Their arms can be above their head or by their side.
- Position yourself in warrior behind them.
- Locate the tops of the muscles, which run about an inch away from the spine from the lowest part of the back all the way up to the neck.
- Locate the sacrum, the flat bone at the very bottom of the low back.

Posture:

- Place your fists or palms (slightly turned out) on either side of the sacrum.
- Make gentle circles with one hand and then the other.
- Use fist chasing fist to ease onto one side of the back at a time.
- Repeat with fist or palm hopping onto the same spot.
- Repeat the three steps of circles, chasing and hopping in different spots moving up the back.
- Continue until you are between the shoulder blades.
- Move above their head and press between the shoulder blades and a couple of spots down the back.
- Return to the original warrior position and massage down to the sacrum.

Benefits:

- Stretches the lower back.
- Stretches the spine.
- Opens the shoulders and neck.
- Opens the hips.
- Helps to wake up your partner.

How slow can you go:

- This is a gentle way to wake up your partner and end the massage with a light stretch.
- Your touch should be light and gradual.
- Begin with circles to ease in the pressure.
- Increase the pressure ever so slowly, paying attention to their body's signals that they are able to relax while the pressure deepens.
- When working both sides of the back at the same time, alternate pressing on each side before you press down with both hands at the same time.

For their safety and comfort:

For partners that have a hard time getting into this position, you'll want to have lots of props on hand. Use pillows to close any large gaps of space. That could include the space between chest and knees as well as the space between their ankles and bum.

If your partner is unable to sit in this position, they can sit on their bum and go into a forward bend. They can sit on a pillow, and you can also place pillows on their lap. Press on their back gently to encourage a forward bend.

For your safety and comfort:

You may try to squat if you find that more comfortable than the warrior pose. When positioning yourself above the head, the goal is to press on the upper back. There is no need to reach all the way to the lower back unless you are much taller than your partner.

On a bed or massage table:

This posture can be done on a bed if you are comfortable getting into warrior stance. To complete the part where you are above their head, you may need to stand at the foot of the bed. If you choose this position, ask your partner to position herself in the child's pose accordingly.

You may need to skip this if massaging on a table that is too narrow for your partner to get into this position.

Big Sweeps

A gentle sweep of the back for added relaxation and an extra sweet ending.

Transition:

Come into warrior or standing.

Posture:

- Use your hands in a sweeping motion for an extensive sweep of the back.
- Spend at least thirty to sixty seconds and sweep in multiple directions.

Benefits:

Relaxes the whole body and back.

How slow can you go:

- Take your time and sweep the whole back: up and down, s-shapes, making circles, and in whatever way inspires you.
- Come back to your original intention and bring any personal touches as you finish the massage.

For their safety and comfort:

Sweeping is such a great way to end the massage, and in this case, spend extra time sweeping out the whole back. But for partners who have a hard time staying in this posture, you could ask them to sit up and then sweep their back.

For your safety and comfort:

Change up the stance so you don't spend too much time in warrior. Try standing or walking around their body.

Ending the Massage

End the massage just as you began, in a prayer position giving thanks to your partner. Feel all the benefits of giving and take some nice deep breaths filled with gratitude and appreciation for this loving connection of compassionate touch.

PART

LOVE: THE SOURCE OF COMPASSIONATE TOUCH

⌘

"If you knew who walked beside you, you would never experience doubt or fear again."

~FROM A COURSE IN MIRACLES

CHAPTER 17

THERE ARE ELEPHANTS IN THE ROOM

Writing this book has been a journey that has taken over a decade. It is part of my central mission on this planet, to make compassionate touch accessible and powerful for anyone who chooses and bring to light the absolute joy of giving massage.

Along the way I've had struggles and triumphs. Some of my struggle has had to do with feeling lost and uncertain about what to do with my life and if a life dedicated to touch was enough. For many years I felt like I could not hear my intuition as I tried to navigate the path of life. Eventually that shifted, and I remember asking as I was going through those challenges why weren't there more books and offerings on this feeling of loneliness and lost-ness.

I read lots of books and learned techniques from many teachers on how to think more positively and connect with Spirit. But it seemed all too easy. Like they were already where I wanted to be, and there was a big gap in between where I sat and what I read.

It's from that place that my poems and writings begin. Words that came to me, that compelled me to put pen in hand while they flowed through me. It's from there that I share with you, and I hold space and I offer some empathy and some love wherever you are on your journey.

There Are Elephants in the Room

Their Names are You and Me.
They are born of wisdom and lost in time
Large Enough to fell a tree with one mighty step.
So easily drunk on their power
That they have forgotten their shadow.
They are scared of the dark
And what the mouse might bring.

There are elephants in the room
And their names are fear and loathing.
They take up so much space
That we forget they are there.
They obscure our truth
We get swallowed up.
Yet we invite them in.
The price we pay is high.
It is every moment clouded over.
It is a lifetime of forgotten regrets.
It is dying with the words "if only" glued to our lips.
Yet the funny thing is, these elephants are born of wisdom
And to talk of them is to be released.

The story they are sharing is "I shall be free"
When we live in truth
When we are no longer afraid to live from the heart
When the depth and beauty of one truly profound moment
Outranks the hopes and dreams of an uncertain future
When we stop making plans
And surrender
To Silence
To Space.

To a morning dove's call
Piercing through the forest resting in our heart
A sound so pure
A tune in perfect pitch
You can't help but embrace what it means to be aligned
And to remember it.
Even as the elephants try to squeeze out our memories.

The pulse, the heart, the beat remains.
The door is opened
Hand in hand
We step into knowingness.

No longer scared of what we find in the shadows
Where the mouse is timeless.
It is patience
It is love
It fills us up.
The elephants remain
But our room is now the whole universe.

CHAPTER 18

A Different Kind of Love Letter

"Even if they don't always know the right words and how to express themselves, believe in the people who show up every day."

~Shai Plonski

Marianne Williamson wrote the *Return to Love: Reflections on a Course in Miracles*. It is a reflection on the teachings called *A Course in Miracles*. It's a life changing book about what happens when you accept God or the power of love into your life on a daily basis.

While reading that book, I happened to come across a song that most of us know so well which is the Beatles "All You Need is Love." Hearing that song after having read that book was as though I was hearing it for the first time. It was as though there was a secret code contained in those lyrics, a message being channeled about the power of love. As such, here I share my reflections on "All You Need is Love."

Love is the sound that is being whispered all around. This is what the Beatles wanted to share in their song, "All You Need Is Love." They had been to the well and back and report that this is the song being played over and over again in the universe. It is the key that both binds and unlocks everything and anything. It is not just lip service. It is the sound that reveals itself to you when you are ready to hear it.

It is a given that anyone can hear it, and it is a given that you can only hear it when the sound wants to sing to you. My experience is that there is some purging, some sacrifice, some of the hero's journey that has to be undertaken without ever hearing it, so you can ready yourself, because a miracle changes your life forever. The roots have to be uprooted just enough so this sound can infiltrate the very fiber of your being.

Life is indeed a game. That means there are rules, and depending on the rules one chooses to adopt, the reality of the game changes.

There is only one rule of love. When in doubt, when you're down, when you're up and all around, love. With that as your mantra the next rules, the next actions are revealed. Love is both an action and an entity. It is that rare creation that is both the cause and the effect.

So, to play the game of love you need a compass. If your compass is dirty, obscured, or broken it needs to be fixed. If you play the game without a functioning compass, a whole lot of frustration will ensue. But at the same time, sometimes a person needs that frustration so they know their compass needs repairs. The compass is your intuition.

When we are children, that compass is our only guide. Too often for so many of us, as we grow we are not taught to protect it, to nurture it, and to value it as much as we should. It often gets discarded or at least dampened as we progress into our teenage years and beyond.

By the time our adult self rediscovers its true value, there is often a lot of energy that needs to be expended to get it up and running again. And sometimes, even if we get it working, it'll still be bound to occasional malfunctions because of years of choices that eventually pop up as present-day karma. Because of the pressures of the world, our parents, our friends, our biology, ourselves that put demands on our time.

If you can't trust or feel your intuition, you are missing the essential tool that love uses to fuel you.

It can be hard to love because we are often conditioned to be results-based on how we live our life and how we expect things to play out. We are linear and scientific. I do A and I expect B. When I get B, I have the proof that my choice, my compass is working. When I don't get those results, then I know that either I am wrong or this whole game is wrong. The latter is what happens when I don't get to B again and again and again.

Then you have to realize, what game are you playing? This is not the game of how to get rich, how to have an easy life, or how to get everything you want. This is the game of learning how to be yourself.

Regardless of what we do or know or see or try or explore, the world or the universe is going to be alright without us. The more you can strike a balance between relaxation and agitation, the more you will be shown, the more that will be known, the more you will be somewhere that you're meant to be.

That is the method to fixing and polishing your compass and learning its language. Keep finding ways every day and in any way that values relaxing above all else. Relaxing is not the same as "vegging out" or mindlessly watching TV. It is unplugging from pressure, but the best kind comes from activities that help us unplug. That means use electronics when necessary or when you need to, but plant the seed in your consciousness that there's a better way. It's in a breath, a stretch, a walk, a hobby, you name it. Once again, when you're used to something else, such as go-go-go, then it's simple to change, but it's not easy.

So here it is. The domain of the inner universe of love and the way forward that helps you to know you is feminine. It is patience, it is gentleness, it is slowness, it is nature, it is depth, it is the speed at which roses come into bloom. Just because we don't sit in front of it to watch it do its thing day after day, doesn't mean it isn't happening.

Eventually, we see the results every time it is nurtured, cared for, tended to with grace. But it is not part of the scientific method where doing A brings you B. Because you have changed. You are no longer A, therefore you can't expect that you're making B. You're making a whole lot of something else, and it's only when you are in it that you realize that you've been making it all along and it sure as heck isn't B. It's a whole lot more than that.

PART IV

STUDENTS' STORIES

⌘

"Folks need to know the ways we change and are changed when we love. It is only by bearing concrete witness to love's transformative power in our daily lives that we can assure those who are fearful that commitment to love will be redemptive, a way to experience salvation."

~BELL HOOKS

In their own words, here are some of the stories students of compassionate touch asked to share. Some of these people have been giving some form of compassionate touch for years, and others for just a few months. I am overwhelmed reading how many people's lives have fundamentally changed from this practice. Their stories are priceless. The wish here is that you find inspiration, motivation, and connection with this loving community who have embraced the power of touch. Let them inspire you to keep giving and learning and see how far the joy of giving massage can take you!

CHAPTER 19

MEET MARY BETH

Why Did You First Get Interested in Studying Thai Massage?

I was interested in massage at an early age and considered studying massage therapy after high school. Instead, I studied dance and strengthened my skills and interest in contemporary and contact improv. Around this time I became more aware of Thai Massage but didn't consider training due to budget. After many years of working in a steady administration job, which I transitioned into from dance for stability, I became injured and totally lost all my mind/body connection and endured long months of recovery, relearning that relationship in a healthy and sustainable way, learning much more about myself. At that time, my heart was seeking new purpose and meaning, and I found it through Thai Massage.

How Long Have You Been Practicing?

I have been practicing Thai Massage for one full year now. In some ways, it feels like much longer, but I continue to learn and grow, and expect I always will.

How Often Do You Massage?

I massage two to six hours a week, and most of my clients see me for two-hour sessions.

How Have You Benefited from Making Massage a Part of Your Life?

Every time I massage, I feel a strong connection to the flow of energy in my client through their energy lines and marma points, which somehow also opens the channels of energy within myself. It is a true pleasure for me to sense blockages of energy in my recipients and release them. I feel a strong sense of gratitude after every massage and am further fulfilled in the gratitude I receive from my recipients afterward. This entire process of practice and response is thoroughly authentic and life giving. While I imagined this practice would be fulfilling, I didn't realize how continually renewing it would be for me.

How Did You Overcome Obstacles to Make Giving Massage a Regular Part of Your Life?

Practice was my biggest obstacle. I felt I should be able to tap into my recipients at a deep level from the very beginning, but this took time, feedback, and patience. It became easier once I became more familiar with the positions, posture, and presses which put me in a flow. I sent out invitations to receive and had a number of willing volunteers who helped me past this time and communicated their boundaries with me.

How Has Massaging Helped Your Relationships, Both Personally and Professionally?

I'm feeling more fulfilled with myself and confident with my ability to provide for myself and others. I find I am less jealous, resentful, and less competitive. There are so many people in our world that don't know how to share healthy and healing touch. I feel being able to offer this power, feel the profound impact of it being received, and sense the process taking place all have a value greater than money, as they are not performed for money but for healing. Any funds that are exchanged in this process are a formality to accommodate the society we live and survive in, but the work is beyond these bounds for me.

It has given me a much better relationship with myself. If find I am most receptive and honoring of the value of my instincts when I practice Thai Massage. I find my recipient's body guides me to where it needs touch and release along the energy lines. I need only listen and respect the laws of leverage in my own body to assist in this release.

What Are Some Benefits You've Seen from People Who Have Received Massage from You?

I often receive comments of gratitude from my recipients. Most recently I received this comment from a first-time client: "I wanted to let you know how much I enjoyed the massage yesterday. Thank you. You have started a whole new conversation in my body and my right hip has not hurt since. Love it."

In fact, I had no idea this seventy-two-year-old woman had pain in her right hip when I started.

Do You Have Someone You Exchange with Regularly? How Has That Helped Your Relationship?

I have one friend I exchange with on a semi-regular basis. He is more of a beginner, and I coach him through presses he gives to me. These are some of the best massages I ever receive, for more than one reason. It is fun for me to describe what I need, to awaken this attention in him, and finally to receive it through his hands (or knees or feet) and heart.

If You Could Tell the World Anything about the Power of Touch and Giving Massage, What Would It Be?

We all need to love and be loved. The assurance and trust provided by healing touch and built upon in stress release, communicates all these sentiments without the complexity of verbal crafting or interpretation.

Where Would You like to See Massage Make Bigger Inroads?

This is a form that draws people to it. They need only hear about it to be interested. Having said that, I believe the elderly, the depressed, the insomniacs, amongst so many others would benefit from this form. Either to give or to receive.

CHAPTER 20

Meet Pamyla

Why Did You First Get Interested in Studying Thai Massage?

I first got interested in Thai Massage as something that could help my daughter. I do energy work, and I was looking for a way to offer loving touch and to help to keep her central nervous system calmer. It quickly became something I offer to clients in the clinic and to friends because of the deep and profound results that keep showing up.

How Long Have You Been Practicing?

I began my Thai Massage training in July 2014.

How Often Do You Massage?

Six days a week.

How Have You Benefited from Making Massage a Part of Your Life?

The principles of Thai Massage have become a way of life. Thai Massage created the space for me to deepen my capacity to be compassionate. Through loving kindness and offering touch from that place deep within me, a space is created to just be with people and myself in our pain or suffering without the "need" to fix anything.

Early in the training of Thai Massage, I had a client with a transformative result from the session, and the relief from pain and the ease in the body brought tears. He asked: "What did you do to me?"

I intuitively sensed the significance of this question this master before me was asking, and just knew the place I came from in answering this question was going to be a game changer. I reflected a moment, and I answered my truth: "I loved you." And the peace and grace that filled up in me was beyond understanding. It could only be felt. And from that moment forward, I became someone new. And to this day, I work at deepening this within me so I have more to offer.

How Did You Overcome Obstacles to Make Giving Massage a Regular Part of Your Life?

Making intuition my first sense, not my sixth sense. I am also fortunate that body work is the way I earn my livelihood, so It is easy for me to make Thai a regular, even daily part of my life.

How Has Massaging Helped Your Relationships, Both Personally and Professionally?

My relationship to my Self has benefitted the most from massaging. As a result, all relationships, both personal and professional, became richer, deeper, and clearer. Massage allows me to build and shape relationships that are more sustainable. Putting the practice of metta into my day more and more has greatly reduced my own suffering. I'm definitely getting more comfortable being uncomfortable, less judgmental of myself and others, and therefore creating less suffering.

What Are Some Benefits You've Seen from People Who Have Received Massage from You?

People have reduced pain, anxiety, and they become calmer, more accepting, and peaceful. Every single person has said they feel more gratitude on a regular basis. Regularly, I hear how this work is helping them to change perspective on events and situations in their lives, and they are gentler and more forgiving. They have an increase in ease and mental well-being.

There is the friend who I did Thai Massage on daily while she was in palliative care. The hockey player who asked, "What did you do to me?" The time I was doing Thai Massage on my daughter while she was on life support. The woman who came in having a panic attack. Those are a few.

If You Could Tell the World Anything about the Power of Touch and Giving Massage, What Would It Be?

We all have times in our life when we wonder if what we do or say matters or makes a difference. Learning to touch in this way will take away any doubt because you will experience and witness miracles and a deeper connection to all of life.

Where Would You like to See Massage Make Bigger Inroads?

I would love to see Thai Massage for self-care taught in schools, specifically high school and university/college. I have been using Thai Massage, and the benefits for mental health and well-being with students who are so stressed, anxiety ridden, and filled with fear they are really challenged to function well. I would love to teach this to students and make it a part of a peer-help program. I know Thai Massage can be incredibly helpful in a crisis, but I also know it could be used as a great prevention tool. The meditative qualities of the massage are really understated and is a significant distinction between this and other types of massage. I would also love to see some brain mapping on the practitioner and the receiver to actually measure these benefits.

Is There Anything Else You'd like to Share?

My mantra and guiding voice is you saying, "How slow can you go? How high can you fly?" It keeps me on track more than you know.

CHAPTER 21

MEET JEFF

Why Did You First Get Interested in Studying Thai Massage?

Originally, I was told that it would be helpful with making adjustments while teaching yoga classes. Now I am finding many beneficial applications that I hadn't realized before.

How Long Have You Been Practicing?

Only for a few months as of now, but I plan on using this for the rest of my life.

How Often Do You Massage?

My wife and I have been trying to massage each other once a week. Some weeks are better than others, but I also try to share it with at least one other person each week, especially those who have never experienced Thai Massage.

How Have You Benefited from Making Massage a Part of Your Life?

I am realizing how much of a mindfulness meditation it can be if you are really focusing on being present to what the receiver's body is telling you. I tend to easily do too much every day and giving Thai Massage helps slow things down for me. I am finding that it is as beneficial to give as it is to receive, just in a different way.

How Did You Overcome Obstacles to Make Giving Massage a Regular Part of Your Life?

My wife and I have a one-year-old at home, and we definitely have to make massaging a priority. So, we decided that once he goes to sleep that would be our best time to get to massage each other. We used to just watch TV to unwind at the end of the day, and now we get to do this instead. I would take an hour massage over an hour of watching TV any day. In fact, I would rather give an hour-long massage then watch an hour of TV now!

How Has Massaging Helped Your Relationships, Both Personally and Professionally?

Personally, it has given my wife and I something that we can do for each other to help better take care of ourselves. I know that when my body feels good, then I am a much kinder, nicer, and compassionate person. The ripple effect of how it can help me is probably immeasurable. Professionally, I am a PE teacher, and I teach a rock-climbing unit. The students always complain about how it hurts their hands and forearms. So, I showed them how to massage a partner's forearms and hands, and they loved it! Now it's part of how we end class after rock climbing!

What Are Some Benefits You've Seen from People Who Have Received Massage from You?

My brother doesn't do a great job of taking care of himself physically (doesn't exercise, sits way too much, and has a poor diet). He is always complaining about his back as well. He let me give him a sixty-minute full-body massage (after a lot of persuasion), and I noticed such a difference in his attitude and demeanor. He usually has a very scattered brain, short attention span, and is very self-absorbed (and yes, I love my brother), but after the massage it was as if a switch was flipped inside him. He was noticeably much more relaxed, attentive, and mindful while we hung out afterward. It was very nice to see how different someone can be when their body feels good and also very rewarding to be able to share that feeling with family.

If You Could Tell the World Anything about the Power of Touch and Giving Massage, What Would It Be?

There is a benefit to touch that can't be explained with words. We are all connected, and when we don't feel connected we start to see that affect our physical, mental, and emotional health. Thai Massage has the ability to help us feel that connection with each other and bring us back to a better state of well-being.

Where Would You like to See Massage Make Bigger Inroads?

I'm already surprised at how easily I've been able to share Thai Massage in so many different capacities. I've been giving individuals Thai Massages, but also incorporating it into my Yin Yoga classes, which my students have loved. I've incorporated it very mildly with my PE classes in our rock-climbing unit and would like to see where else this could be incorporated. Also, I'm very involved in the CrossFit community, and I was able to give the owner of my gym Thai Massage. He was excited about how it helped him with his recovery process from the intense workouts that he does. He immediately started asking how he could learn to do Thai Massage to help his athletes after training sessions. I would love to be able to share something like this with more athletes and teach them how they could massage each other after workouts to help recover faster.

Is There Anything Else You'd like to Share?

Thank you for sharing this with me and particularly not just showing us the technique and the massage sequence but emphasizing the first pillar: metta. I find that as long as I am connected with this first pillar, the massage comes naturally and is enjoyable to give.

CHAPTER 22

MY VOICE IS TOUCH

Why touch? Isn't that soft, isn't that weak? Is it weak to be vulnerable? Or is vulnerability where our greatest strengths live? It is vulnerable if to touch is to feel, and what you feel is love. And what you want is to feel your heart burst onto the world. To help someone in need, in pain, or someone who simply wants to relax.

There are many ways to help and some are a lot harder than they seem. Touch is not one of them. We do it every day and all the time. What's the big deal?

Right. Is it a big deal to touch someone with care, someone you love, someone you've never met except you've seen that smile or that frown a million times before?

Damn right it's a big deal if you think about it. What is being touched? Who is doing the touching? What is involved? When you touch your mother and you think about her beloved mother who was once your grandmother who played a part in raising not only you and her, but a million others who crossed her path, do you think that means something more, something less than what it is?

When you touch, you come to life. When you touch, you prove Descartes wrong as wrong can be. He said, "I think, therefore I am." But it is not about thinking, it is about being. Touching transports us to the place where we know. Where the whole is greater than the sum of its parts, and there is a chance for something greater still. Where peace can flourish and hate can disappear. Where there are no judgements, no anger, no love, no need for that brotherhood of man.

Mr. Lennon pressed a simple key out of eighty-eight, and we knew what he meant. We were touched. So, yes, when you touch, you give back, you receive, you make music, you sing high, you get into the flow of life where the infinite reigns supreme.

So remind yourself of how awesome you are, your mother, your son, your daughter, and the baker down the street. Take away someone's tensions or pain, make them smile in a way they haven't before, and be that change you want to see and be and need.

Know that you can make a difference every single day. And if you do touch as many days as possible between now and forever, then who does that change? You? Her? Him? Everyone? My voice is touch, and I know you. Your voice is touch and you know me, so how about we get together and figure this out?

Isn't it about time we understand that touch is not a skill, it's a birthright. It lives in love, in compassion, in your smile and in mine, and from there it grows through our fingers and our toes, outward from our knees to the word please, and we can all do it.

My voice is touch because when that is the language I speak, I don't care about the news. I know that anger, and hate and killing are gone, and when you know it then it's doubly true. And here I am so ready to share it with you.

Now stop thinking touch is a skill you can live without, or that you have to pay to know, or that you can't do it, or only professionals have what it takes. That is just not true. Everyone can, everyone should, and it's only a matter of what? Who? How many? Your lover? Your mother? Your father, your son, your daughter? Your best friend dying of cancer looking for a few more moments of dignity? Your fill-in-the-blank who you care about or who you want to show you care.

So why not show 'em what you've got when what you've got is full of life and the power to touch.

My voice is touch, and I can't wait to share it with you.

Bonus Video Lessons

Get the accompanying videos for every massage technique taught in this course here: **www.stillightcentre.com/thaimassagemadesimple**

RESOURCES

Marianne Williamson, *Return to Love: Reflections on the Principles of A Course in Miracles*

Rainer Maria Rilke, *Letters to a Young Poet*

Max Storm, *There Is No App for Happiness: How to Find Joy and Fulfillment in the Digital Age*

Marcus Aurelius, *Meditations*

Pema Chodron, *When Things Fall Apart: Heart Advice for Difficult Times*

Vipassana Meditation, www.Dhamma.org

Omega Institute, Rhinebeck, New York

Wayne Dyer, *I Can See Clearly Now*

Adam Gopnik, *Feel Me: What the Science of Touch Says About Ourselves,* New Yorker Magazine

Dacher Keltner, Inside Out Pixar's Movie

Mark Twain, *The Lowest Animal an Essay*

Jalaluddin Rumi, *13th Century Sufi mystic*

Thichi Nhat Hanh, Official website PlumVillage.org

Jill Bolte Taylor, TED Talks *My Stroke of Insight*

Alexis Mulhauser, Nia.com

Dan Gilbert, TED Talks *The Surprising Science of Happiness*

Helen Schucman, *A Course in Miracles*

Bell Hooks, *Creating a Culture of Love*

SPECIAL FACEBOOK GROUP

Come and join our Facebook group made specially for readers like you who want to jump in and learn to give massage to better your life and those around you. You are likely to massage people of different ages, body types, issues. This page brings people together from around the world to help support one another, share your success stories, and provide tips on how to help take care of your body while giving the best massage possible.

This is the best place to ask me questions as well for timely and helpful advice.

Come join us here on Facebook:
www.facebook.com/groups/CompassionateTouch

ACKNOWLEDGEMENTS

Mutual support is one of the nine principles for living a harmonious life. It is also what fills me up when I take a moment to reflect on all the people who have come together dedicating their time, love, and energy to help bring this book to life.

Having a daughter, I know well how the expression "it takes a village" applies. A similar effort is true when bringing a book into the world, and I have one incredible village.

My family, including my mom, brother, sister, and all their partners who have challenged me my whole life to help bring out a better version of me.

The amazing team at TCK Publishing including my amazing project manager Sarah Dyck, incredible editor Jennifer Crosswhite, and the wonderful Tom Corson-Knowles. Such gratitude and appreciation for all that you do to support writers and artists to make their dreams come true.

Thousands of students and some wonderful friends—who are also all my teachers—have provided insight, guidance, support and inspiration in crafting the massage flow, sharing their energy, and providing all kinds of invaluable feedback to help me find ways to communicate the messages here that I could have never done on my own.

That includes my sister Sharri, who helped edit an early version of the book; Sarah for helping to illuminate my path in such a radiant way; Ananya for your partnership, wisdom and faith, in dancing together on this path; Alexis, who provided so many helpful ideas and tons of feedback; Kate, who helped plant the seed that became this book. Joanne, who has been a bedrock of support as we grow our school.

Pamyla, Jeff, Anne, Joanne, and Mary Beth for sharing their stories. Peter, Louisa, Pam, Adrian, Mark, Melanie, Donna, Bob, Krista, Alissa, Carie, Cheryl, Jessica, Michelle, Tara, Tiffany, Tsu Ching, and Gloria, for reading advanced copies in record time and sharing all kinds of helpful advice that I think makes this book exponentially better. George, for his support as my first student at Still Light Centre and now a wonderful teacher in his own right who's been with me since the very beginning.

I have had so many wonderful massage and yoga teachers guide me in my craft, and I am honored to have learned from some of the best in Kam Thye Chow, Deanna Villa, Kaline Kelly, Ariela Grodner, Rick Gold, Danny Paradise and Dr. Madan Bali. You are all shining lights, teaching me more than you'll ever know.

What this whole process has taught me above all else is that these techniques and these words are not mine, not in the least. They are gifts from love, from metta—the spirit of loving kindness and compassion— and my wish all along has been to share the message. I pray I've served them well.

ABOUT THE AUTHOR

Shai Plonski has taught Thai Massage to more than 3,300 people on three continents for the past fifteen years. He has written or co-written fifteen books and manuals on the art of this practice. Shai loves educating other people on how giving massage is a life-changing choice and sharing how simple and easy it is to do.

Shai is the founder of the Still Light Centre School of Thai Massage. Our centre is based in Hamilton Ontario, about an hour from Toronto. We are also invited to teach all over the world. For Shai and the team's upcoming workshops please visit: **www.stillightcentre.com/category/courses-calendar**

To invite Shai or a member of the team to come teach a workshop at your studio or center please email us: **info@stillightcentre.com**

Get free guidance on how to give compassionate touch and Thai Massage online by visiting: **shaiplonski.sendlane.com/view/compassionate-touch-landing-page.**

Learn more at **www.stillightcentre.com**

CONNECT WITH SHAI

Thank you so much for making the time to read this book and bring compassionate touch into your life and into the lives of those you care for. I'm excited for you to start your path of giving massage and how it will help improve your health and relationships.

If you have any questions, feel free to contact me at **www.stillightcentre.com/get-in-touch**

Connect with me on Facebook at **www.facebook.com/shaiploski** and Instagram at **www.instagram.com/shaiplonski**

Check out my massage blog and the latest updates by visiting: **www.stillightcentre.com**

I'm wishing you incredible health and happiness—now and every day.

Much love and metta,

Shai

OTHER BOOKS BY SHAI PLONSKI

Thai Massage: Unlocking the Secrets to Universal Touch

Couples Thai Massage

Thai Massage for Pregnancy and the Elderly: The Soft Approach

Thai Massage for Restorative Yoga Teachers

These books and more Thai Massage manuals are available by contacting us directly at: **info@stillightcentre.com**

BOOK DISCOUNTS AND SPECIAL DEALS

Sign up for free to get discounts and special deals on our bestselling books at

www.TCKpublishing.com/bookdeals

ONE LAST THING...

Thank you for reading! If you enjoyed this book or found it useful, I'd be very grateful if you'd post a short review on Amazon. I read every comment personally and am always learning how to make this book even better. Your support really does make a difference.

Search for *The Joy of Giving a Massage* by Shai Plonski to leave your review.

Thanks again for your support!

www.ingramcontent.com/pod-product-compliance
Lightning Source LLC
Chambersburg PA
CBHW070059080526
44586CB00013B/1127